LAW
BASICS
Student Study Guides

DELICT

FIFTH EDITION

LAW
BASICS
Student Study Guides

DELICT

FIFTH EDITION

By

Gordon Cameron, LLB (Hons) MSc

Senior Lecturer in Law at the University of Dundee

W. GREEN

THOMSON REUTERS

First Edition published in 2002

Published in 2019 by Thomson Reuters,
trading as W. Green, 21 Alva Street, Edinburgh, EH2 4PS.
Thomson Reuters is registered in England & Wales, Company
No.1679046.
Registered Office and address for service: 5 Canada Square, Canary
Wharf, London, E14 5AQ.

Computerset by W. Green
Printed and bound by CPI Group (UK) Ltd, Croydon, CR0 4YY

No natural forests were destroyed to make this product:
only farmed timber was used and replanted.

A CIP catalogue record of this book is available from the British Library.

ISBN 978-0-414-06472-0

For orders, go to: *http://www.tr.com/uki-legal-contact*;
Tel: 0345 600 9355.

For further information on our products and services, visit
http://www.sweetandmaxwell.co.uk/wgreen

Thomson Reuters, the Thomson Reuters logo and W. GREEN are
trademarks of Thomson Reuters.

© 2019 Thomson Reuters

In memoriam, Bill Stewart 1958–2010

CONTENTS

TABLE OF CASES

1. INTRODUCTION

The place of delict in the general scheme of things

The origins of delict lie in a concern to maintain good order. Historically, **1–01** the vengeance or blood feud that would otherwise follow from some wrong done could be bought off by providing for money to be paid by the perpetrator to the victim or the victim's family. This was a device intended to discourage citizens from taking the law into their own hands and to provide a more civilised alterative to lawless feud than the old *ius talionis*, an eye for an eye and a tooth for a tooth. The early tendency was to provide a tariff of compensation or penalties to be paid according to the injury done. Penalties varied in some cases with the status of the victim. The law of delict starts to develop with deliberate and wilful wrongs such as maiming, slaughter, theft, robbery and insult. In the modern law, a clear separation from criminal law is established, but historically this distinction was not always so clearly drawn. Modern criminal law is mobilised by public authorities and the result of a successful prosecution is punishment of the offender. The law of delict is mobilised by the individual or corporate body seeking compensation for loss suffered or to prevent harm from arising. Criminal law punishes, delict compensates or prevents. However, the underlying idea to maintain good order remains common to both criminal law and delict though the point may appear more obvious in the former case.

Delict belongs within Scots private law. It is a branch of the law of obligations. An obligation can be understood as a bond linking two persons. The obligation in delict is to make reparation, that is to repair the loss by payment of damages. This obligation arises from wrongdoing, so the law imposes on the wrongdoer (the defender) an obligation to pay damages to his victim (the pursuer). Where an obligation to make reparation is recognised, the pursuer acquires the right to damages against the defender. The counter-part of this right is the duty that falls on the defender to pay the sum. Where liability in reparation is established, the court will order such an award.

The question at the heart of delict, then is whether or not the defender is liable to the pursuer in damages. Note, however, that this is not the only question that courts may be asked to address. The defender may admit liability but dispute its extent so, for example, the parties will argue over quantum, that is the sum of damages payable. Equally, the action may not be for damages at all, but some other remedy such as interdict against a wrong that is anticipated. The party seeking an interdict is the petitioner who brings proceedings against the respondent.

Most delictual disputes are settled outside court, either before or after litigation proceedings have been initiated. Solicitors negotiate on the part of their clients and seek to obtain settlement from the other party. This process of negotiation depends on the relative strengths and weaknesses of the pursuer and defender's positions. If the pursuer's position is sufficiently strong, that is they have a reasonable chance of getting at least some of what they are after should the case come to court, then the defender can normally be persuaded to negotiate. The defender ought to settle when it becomes apparent that the pursuer's claim is bound to succeed. Equally, the client with a hopeless case should not be advised to pursue. When disputes become clear cut like this, persisting in an argument that cannot be won is likely to prove an expensive mistake since the further negotiation and litigation proceed, the more the expenses rack up, and the general rule of thumb is that the winner recovers the expenses of the action from the loser.

A solicitor then, must develop expertise in communication and negotiation plus knowledge and experience of the litigation process if they are to have any chance of obtaining a satisfactory outcome for their client. The process of acting for a client must, however, start with an evaluation of the client's position and for that, a knowledge and understanding of the law is required. Essentially, it is this ability that is tested in private law exams, especially through the medium of problem questions. The student is presented with a factual scenario and is required to provide an analysis. This anticipates the situation whereby the solicitor gleans information from a client, directly or via a written record of a client consultation or telephone call, and determines from that the best way to proceed. In either case, the legally significant facts must be identified and an opinion formed on how the law applies in the circumstances. The solicitor will know the law and when the possible application of the law to the circumstances is unclear, will research the law and form an opinion, or ask advice of another lawyer, for example by instructing counsel for an opinion. The student must demonstrate sufficient knowledge of those elements of the law covered in the syllabus to make relevant observations and to address any specific questions posed by the examiners. The student is not expected to be an expert, but ought to aim for a broad overview of the subject with a firm grasp of key points and should work to clear up any matters of major confusion before presenting for examination.

General principle of delictual liability

1–02 Delictual liability can be understood with reference to a single general principle. This is expressed *dammum injuria datum*, which can be translated as "loss caused unlawfully, without justification or wrongfully", but is probably best left in the original Latin. No obligation to make reparation arises without some form of loss. The term "loss" is used here in a very broad sense. Loss indicates some diminution and, while that can refer to money or damage to other property, it can also encompass forms of harm such as personal injury or death and more abstract things like harm to reputation. The law recognises certain interests as protected. These interests may be presented under four broad headings: protection of the person; protection of liberty; protection of reputation; and protection of interests in property. Any unjustified and non-trivial invasion of a protected interest amounts to a loss. There is no such thing as a victimless delict and wrongdoers may act as wrongfully as they wish without incurring liability unless there is some person or body who suffers loss as a consequence. Since an obligation is a bond linking two persons; a victim as well as a perpetrator (delinquent or wrongdoer) is required for its existence. There is always a creditor in an obligation—the person with the right being the creditor, the person under the duty being the debtor.

If the obligation to make reparation arises from wrongdoing it follows that losses arising without any wrong having been done are not reparable. This situation may be described as *damnum absque injuria* (alternatively expressed *damnum sine injuria*), that is loss without a wrong, and in such circumstances the loss must lie where it falls. Alternatively, such losses may be recovered through some means other than recourse to the law of delict, an action for breach of contract for instance, but without a wrong there will be no liability in delict. An award of damages can be seen as shifting the loss from the person who has suffered it onto the person who must, at law, take responsibility for causing it. Forming an opinion then, on whether liability arises, is dependent on the lawyer's ability to differentiate between circumstances that will give rise to liability, circumstances that will not and circumstances where the outcome is uncertain or arguable. In arriving at a conclusion, potential arguments must be identified and evaluated in terms of strengths and weaknesses. The study of delict should be geared towards developing such abilities. Only after potential liability has been determined, one way or another, should the focus of attention shift to whether there may be defences available and while it is for the defender to establish any defence, the possibility of defences must also be anticipated on the pursuer's behalf. Of course, if there is no potential liability, there is no need to consider defences.

If losses are to be compensated, that is if the liability of the defender to the pursuer is to be recognised, then this must be justified. Courts can't just re-distribute persons' assets willy-nilly—they must provide just outcomes. First, the pursuer's loss must be attributable to the defender's conduct: the defender can only be required to compensate losses for which they are responsible. Thus, the pursuer must establish that the loss was caused by the defender. For convenience, the rules of causation are presented in the chapter on negligence, although the requirement for causation extends right across delict. In the general case, causation is a necessary, but not a sufficient condition for imposing liability. Accidents will happen and, in addition to causative responsibility, we tend to look also for some element of blameworthiness before making a party liable. Thus, there is no liability where harm follows an involuntary act (see e.g. *Waugh v James K Allen Ltd*) and, broadly speaking, those who cannot be blamed for their conduct may be found to lack the capacity to be held liable. To incur liability the conduct that caused the loss must be, in some sense, wrongful.

Given its centrality to delictual liability, wrongfulness is a surprisingly underdeveloped concept in Scots law. The practice is to regard the requirement of wrongfulness satisfied where the defender's conduct can be shown to be culpable, meaning that the defender is at fault. Liability can, however, arise in certain circumstances without any need for *culpa*, that is fault, to be established, and in such cases liability is said to be strict. Strict liability is the exception rather than the rule. It may be imposed by Parliament through statute, but it also arises in some instances at common law, for example in vicarious liability or defamation. Where liability is strict, culpable conduct is not a necessary condition for the obligation to make reparation. Viewed this way, wrongfulness is a broader concept than *culpa* since culpable conduct is always wrongful but wrongfulness can be recognised without *culpa*. While we cannot always say that delictual liability arises from *culpa*, we can generally say that it arises from harm imposed wrongfully, without right or justification. This is why it was suggested above that *damnum injuria datum* may best be left in Latin. The word *injuria* has the advantage that it can capture within its various nuances of meaning forms of statutory and strict liability for which *culpa* is not required. Finally, where the invasion of an interest can be justified, this will normally afford a defence whether liability arises at common law or under statute. Justifiable invasions are not wrongful, but clearly the scope for justifying any given invasion must be restricted to very specific circumstances.

Culpa

1–03 *Culpa* simply means fault. Historically, when the law of delict comprised specific wrongs (nominate delicts), all of which involved deliberate wrongdoing, there was not very much need to develop the concept of *culpa*. Generally speaking, it is only when the law begins to compensate indirectly caused harm and, very broadly speaking, accidentally caused harm, that fault begins to play a necessary role. The elevation of *culpa* to a central role in delictual liability has been attributed by Professor Geoffrey MacCormack largely to the judgments of Lord President Inglis during the latter part of the 19th century, but the move to fault-based liability around this time is found generally across Western jurisdictions. Professor Reinhard Zimmermann has noted a tendency in jurisdictions that insist on fault to retain elements of strict liability "in disguise" and this is true of Scots law.

Initially, *culpa* was seen as synonymous with negligence corresponding to the old Roman distinction between *culpa* on the one hand and *dolus* (meaning fraud, but also encompassing malice and *animus* injuriandi— intent to injure) on the other. In older texts and case reports, *culpa* is used to mean negligence. Negligence broadly means failure to take care in circumstances where care is required to avoid harm to others or their property. The term *culpa* has, however, been judicially discussed relatively recently in the context of nuisance and must now be understood as a generic term of which negligence is simply a species. Other species of *culpa* are: malice (connoting *animus injuriandi* in which harm to the victim is the intended consequence of the defender's conduct); intention (in which the conduct is deliberately carried out in the knowledge that harm to the victim or their property will be the result); recklessness (another under-developed concept in Scots law, but generally indicating indifference on the part of the defenders to the consequence for others of their actions); and conduct causing a special risk of abnormal damage. This formulation of *culpa* derives from the opinion of Lord President Hope in *Kennedy v Glenbelle* in the process of rejecting an argument to the effect that in order to establish *culpa* the pursuer must establish negligence. There is more than one way of skinning a cat and there is more than one way of establishing *culpa*. But this formulation is not above criticism and for most purposes the classic division between intentionally caused harm and unintentionally caused harm (negligence) suffices. This is so because, while lawyers have to differentiate between cases that proceed on grounds of negligence and cases that proceed on other grounds, most of these other grounds have accepted requirements for liability of their own and, of course, these requirements must be learned. If a case on a specific ground is established, it isn't usually necessary to spell out the form taken by *culpa*, though this is normally possible. That said, bringing a case where loss is caused wrongfully has never, in Scots law, depended on fitting the case into an established category (ground) so an understanding of what is meant by culpability may prove useful. The other side of the coin is that where liability is not strict, the absence of *culpa* should afford a defence.

GENERAL MATTERS

Capacity

The general rule is stated by Erskine thus:

1–04

> "Everyone who has the exercise of reason, and so can distinguish between right and wrong, is naturally obliged to make up the damage befalling his neighbour from a wrong committed by himself."

It follows that capacity may need to be considered as an issue where wrongdoers are incapable adults or children. It is well established that a lack of mental capacity is inconsistent with culpa and so a suit against a (mentally) incapable person would most likely prove fruitless. Scots law, like English law, does not make parents liable for the delicts of their children. The capacity of children for delictual liability is a common law matter, but Scots law sets no age requirement and there is next to no relevant Scots case law. The rule has been expressed by Professor Kenneth Norrie as "neminem in delictis aetis excusat", age itself excuses nobody in delict. Some tempering of standards may, however, be appropriate when dealing with children. Certainly, in common law jurisdictions courts have maintained an objective perspective when considering whether a juvenile defendant ought to have foreseen a particular risk, but have modified this by asking what a reasonable person of roughly the age of the defendant would have foreseen. In this way a 12-year-old boy was held not liable to have foreseen the possibility of a ricochet when launching a sharpened steel rod (*McHale v Watson*) and a 15-year-old girl not to have acted carelessly when "swordfighting" with rulers (*Mullin v Richards*). This approach is broadly consistent with Scots law authority on capacity of children for contributory negligence, although Scottish courts have shown a greater willingness to take into account subjective elements of the individual child, particularly where younger children are concerned. The question that may be asked is whether the child in question would have appreciated the particular danger to which he or she was exposed. This view derives from *Campbell v Ord and Maddison* in which a three-year-old boy had had his hand crushed in agricultural machinery left unattended in the market place in Hawick:

> "It would be as unsound to say as a proposition in law that this child was not capable of negligence as to say that he was. Negligence implies a capacity to apprehend intelligently the duty, obligation, or precaution neglected, and that depends to a large degree on the nature of that which is neglected, as well as on the intelligence and maturity of the person said to have neglected it. The capacity to neglect is a question of fact in the individual case, as much so as to negligence itself, which is always a question of fact…He is no more to be held to have capacity which he had not than to have inches or strength which he had not. If the child was in point of fact unable from his tender years to appreciate the danger, to find the reverse would be contrary to the fact … this question of capacity is one of degree and circumstances, and as such a simple question of fact for a jury" (*Campbell v Ord and Madison* (1873) 1 R 149, per LJC Moncreiff at 153–154).

Finally, unincorporated associations lack legal capacity per se. Nevertheless, it is possible to name such an association as defender, but problems may arise with enforcing actions. It may be better to raise actions against office holders or other members personally. This approach will only succeed, however, where it can be shown that the defender is personally liable to the pursuer in her individual capacity. Personal liability cannot derive purely from the fact of membership or office holding. This was affirmed in *Taylor v Quigley*. While unincorporated associations or clubs may be found liable to third parties they cannot be sued by their own members. Since the liability of a club is joint and several, meaning that all members may be held liable for club debts, effectively club members would be liable to themselves, which is incoherent and impermissible (*Harrison v West of Scotland Kart Club*). Unincorporated associations may incur vicarious liability where the acts of members harm third parties, but there can be no vicarious liability between members. Similarly, as occupiers of premises, an association may be liable to third parties under the Occupiers' Liability (Scotland) Act 1960, but cannot be liable to a member who will be an occupier equally with the other members.

Joint liability

The basis for liability is expressed in the maxim, *culpa tenet suos auctores* **1–05** (fault attaches to its authors). There are, however, circumstances in which more than one party may be liable for causing the same loss. Liability may be vicarious. This means that one party is liable for the delict of another without the first party having been directly involved in the wrongdoing. Classically, vicarious liability attaches to the employer of a person who has committed a delict while carrying out the duties of their employment. Many of the cases covered in this book involve vicarious liability. Vicarious liability is discussed in some detail in Ch.7. Joint fault arises where there is more than one defender responsible for the same delict. The pursuer may elect to sue only one defender and if successful may not also sue the other. There is, however a right of relief exercisable by a party who has settled a claim for damages exercisable against any other joint wrongdoers who might have been found liable had they been sued. In such a case the court will determine a just level of contribution under s.3(2) of the Law Reform (Miscellaneous Provisions) (Scotland) Act 1940. If the party sued has become bankrupt and unable to pay damages the pursuer may sue other wrongdoers, but may not do so where damages have been paid since the pursuer cannot recover damages more than once in respect of the same delict. Where more than one wrongdoer is sued and found liable, the court will award a joint and several decree. Joint and several liability means that the defenders contribute to damages in such proportions as deemed just by the court. The pursuer may recover the full sum in damages from one defender who may in turn recover contributions pro-rata from the other parties found liable (Law Reform (Miscellaneous Provisions) (Scotland) Act 1940 s.3(1)). Finally, liability may be joint without also being several. In such a case, each defender is liable to the pursuer only to the extent of their own liability as determined by the court. An example may be found in *Barker v Corus*, discussed in Ch.2.

2. NEGLIGENCE I: THE GENERAL CASE

Introduction to negligence

2–01 There is no delict of negligence as such. In Scots law, liability for negligence can be seen as the application of the general principle, *damnum injuria datum* in the specific context of unintentionally caused harm. Negligence, as noted earlier, is a specific form of *culpa*. Imposing liability on persons who, broadly speaking, have caused loss accidentally involves considerations that do not apply to the same extent in intentionally caused harm. Unlike fraud, say or assault, conduct giving rise to liability in an action grounded on negligence is not normally wrongful per se, but only becomes characterised in this way when there are harmful effects on others. The intentional actor is more or less certain to cause harm whereas the negligent party has only created a risk of harm that could be avoided with sufficient care. It is uncontentious that a party who deliberately harms another should compensate the loss caused. The negligent actor may not have taken the precautions that they ought, but arguably should be considered less culpable than the intentional actor. With negligently inflicted harm, the case for letting the loss lie where it has fallen is therefore stronger. On the other hand, where the victim has suffered harm through no fault of their own and where that harm is attributable to the defender's conduct, compensation is in principle justifiable. Liability for negligent conduct then, must be kept within bounds. The underlying concern is to avoid "liability in an indeterminate amount for an indeterminate time, to an indeterminate class" (Cardozo J in the US Supreme Court case *Ultramares Corporation v Touche*). There has to be some proportionality between the extent of the defender's wrongdoing and the extent of their liability in damages.

Such concerns are addressed by the concept of the duty of care that operates in negligence, but has no necessary application to intentional wrongdoing. Professor Joe Thomson's characterisation of the duty of care as "a threshold device" is apt. The existence of a duty of care does not of itself determine liability, there are other elements to be established, but it is an essential pre-requisite to the success of any claim grounded on negligence. By recognising duties of care in some cases and not in others, court differentiate between circumstances where defenders must compensate losses and those where losses will be left to lie where they fall. Such decisions are always informed by considerations of fairness and justice, whether these factors are addressed explicitly or not.

The first step in the analysis of negligence is to determine whether the defender owed the pursuer a duty of care. If not, there can be no liability in negligence. If a duty is recognised in the circumstances then there may be liability and the next step is to enquire whether the duty has been breached. Without breach, there is no *culpa* and therefore no liability. Where breach is established, the next step is to enquire whether the breach caused the loss complained of. If not, there is no liability. Where it is established that the breach did cause the loss, the next step is to consider whether all or any of the losses complained of are too remote. Losses that are too remote a consequence of the defender's wrongful conduct (breach of duty) will not be compensated. These are the fundamental elements of liability for negligence and they will be considered in greater detail in the following text.

Finally, the more observant reader will have noticed that there are two chapters on negligence in this book. The present chapter convers the standard case at common law, that is where the loss complained of is personal injury, death or property harm caused by positive conduct on the defender's part. The question of duty is relatively straightforward in these circumstances. The next chapter covers circumstances where special rules or considerations apply because of the absence of precedent, the form taken by the loss, the way in which the loss has been incurred or where the defender is a public body.

THE DUTY OF CARE

The duty of care: general

While the need for a duty of care was already established in Scots law, the **2–02** starting point for the modern law is the case of *Donoghue v Stevenson*, in which the pursuer allegedly suffered severe gastro-enteritis after a decomposing snail emerged from an opaque bottle of "ginger" that she was pouring over her ice cream. This may have been ginger beer. Equally, the term "ginger" may have been used in the generic sense in which it is still used in the West of Scotland. Mrs Donoghue's stomach complaint arose from the fact she had already consumed some of the contents of the bottle. She sought to hold the manufacturer liable to her in damages.

Mrs Donoghue had no right of action in contract since she had no contract with the manufacturer. Moreover, she had no contract with the café owner since the drink had been bought for her by her friend. The House of Lords upheld the view of the Inner House that she had a relevant claim in delict. In a famous passage, Lord Atkin formulated what has become known as the neighbourhood principle. This has become the basis for the modern law of negligence.

> "The liability for negligence, whether you style it such or treat it as in other systems as a species of 'culpa', is no doubt based upon a general public sentiment of moral wrongdoing for which the offender must pay. But acts or omissions which any moral code would censure cannot, in a practical world, be treated so as to give a right to every person injured by them, to demand relief. In this way, rules of law arise which limit the range of complainants and the extent of their remedy. The rule that you are to love your neighbour becomes in law, you must not injure your neighbour; and the lawyer's question, Who is my neighbour? receives

a restricted reply. You must take reasonable care to avoid acts or omissions which you can reasonably foresee would be likely to injure your neighbour. Who, then, in law, is my neighbour? The answer seems to be—persons who are so closely and directly affected by my act that I ought reasonably to have them in contemplation when I am directing my mind to the acts or omissions which are called into question."

The neighbourhood principle imposes on us all a duty to consider the potential effects on others of our conduct and to avoid causing harm by taking the precautions needed in the circumstances. The duty does not require that the potential for harm should be negated completely; compliance with the duty is achieved where reasonable care is taken to guard others against the risks created in the course of activity. While Lord Atkin spoke in terms of acts and omissions—which can be brought together in the term "conduct"—there is in general no liability for pure omissions. This means that people are in general under no duty to guard others against risks that they have not themselves created. If A strikes a golf ball and it is heading in the direction of B then A must shout "fore" to warn B to take avoiding action, since shouting a warning is the appropriate precaution in the context of golf. By contrast, if A is a mere observer and the wayward ball has been struck by C, then A is under no duty to warn B. In this case A is at liberty to stand back and watch the ball strike B and cannot be called upon to compensate B. Any compensation will come from C. Duties in respect of omissions generally only arise either where imposed by statute, where the defender can be said to have assumed responsibility for the interests of the pursuer, where the defender has created the danger or where there is a precedent clearly in point. That said, the following dictum of Lord President Dunedin in *Morton v Dixon* in 1909 seems open to other possibilities:

"Where the negligence of the employer consists of what I may call a fault of omission, I think it is absolutely necessary that the proof of that fault of omission should be one of two kinds, either—to shew that the thing which he did not do was a thing which was commonly done by other persons in like circumstances, or—to shew that it was a thing which was so obviously wanted that it would be folly in anyone to neglect to provide it."

Faced with a potential action grounded on negligence the question of whether the defender owed the pursuer a duty of care must be addressed. The question resolves into two related issues: not only must the defender have owed the pursuer a duty of care, but the harm complained of must have been within the scope of the duty.

To whom is a duty owed?

2–03 Most personal injury litigation arises from incidents on the roads or at work. In such cases the existence of a duty of care owed by pursuer to defender is seldom in doubt. The same may be said for most structured relationships that are well served by precedent. While the existence of a duty must always be averred in pleadings the question only really needs to be addressed in detail in cases where the point is contentious. The neighbourhood principle determines that duties of care are owed to "neighbours in law" and these people are those who ought to be within our contemplation as being likely to be affected by our conduct. This really begs a further question. How can we differentiate those who ought to be within contemplation and to whom therefore a duty is owed from those who might reasonably be overlooked without consequence? Some assistance in addressing this point is provided by Lord MacMillan in a further Scottish appeal to the House of Lords, *Bourhill v Young*.

> "The duty of care is not owed to the world at large, but to those to whom injury may reasonably and probably be anticipated if the duty is not observed."

The question of duty is readily answered where there has been an assumption of responsibility by the defender towards a person or group, otherwise the concept of proximity provides further guidance. Proximity can be an elusive concept when one tries to pin it down, but broadly it refers to factors that tend to draw the pursuer and defender closer so that it becomes easier to say that the defender ought to have had potential loss or harm to the pursuer within his or her contemplation. The key factor in *Donoghue* that supplied proximity was the fact that the drink was provided in an opaque bottle. Because of this, once it left the manufacturer's premises there was no opportunity for anyone to inspect it until it was opened by the consumer. This served to link the defender directly with the pursuer. Thus, the manufacturer and consumer were found to be in a proximate relationship whereby the manufacturer ought to have had the consumer within his contemplation.

The simplest aspect of proximity is spatial or geographic. When undertaking some potentially hazardous physical activity, juggling with chainsaws for instance, a duty of care is owed to persons nearby—persons in the immediate vicinity of the act—who might foreseeably be injured. No duty will be owed to persons outwith the distance over which a chainsaw may be thrown. In *Bourhill v Young* a fishwife claimed that she had suffered nervous shock resulting in miscarriage when she heard the sound of a collision between a motorcycle and a car and later saw blood on the road. While it was accepted that the negligent motorcyclist owed a duty of care to other road users and pedestrians in the vicinity, Mrs Bourhill was at the far side of a tram when the accident occurred and was placed in no danger herself. Her case failed. The motorcyclist could not have foreseen injury to a pedestrian who was so far from events and so the action failed for lack of proximity. Mrs Bourhill herself was outwith the geographical area within which a duty of care was owed.

The idea of proximity is not, however, restricted to its spatial aspect. Proximity may be established by the defender's knowledge of the pursuer, either as an individual or as a member of a well-defined group or class, as being within the range of potential harm. This side of proximity may be illustrated with reference to *Hill v Chief Constable of West Yorkshire*. The police had admitted to mistakes during their investigations into murders committed by serial killer Peter Sutcliffe, notorious as the "Yorkshire Ripper". Jacqueline Hill was Sutcliffe's final victim. Following the death of her daughter, Jacqueline's mother sued, alleging that the police were negligent in failing to identify and apprehend Sutcliffe prior to the murder of Jacqueline. The case was unsuccessful. While it was reasonably foreseeable to the police that young women in the Leeds area were in danger so long as Sutcliffe remained at large, no duty of care was owed to Jacqueline Hill in particular. There was nothing to alert the police to the danger that awaited Jacqueline as an individual and, as one woman in a large population, she was not within a sufficiently well-defined class of persons for a duty to be owed her. There was no element of proximity to link the victim with the police so that she ought to have been within their contemplation. It may be noted in addition that *Hill* also involved an omission: the complaint against the police was that they had failed to deal with a source of danger that they had not themselves created. There was, moreover, a policy argument against recognition of a duty of care in the circumstances. The view was taken that in the process of a criminal investigation, the responsible officers should be free to make decisions according to their professional judgment without the constraint of having to protect their own backs against litigation. Returning briefly to *Donoghue*, policy arguments were aired in that case too. Lord Atkin spoke in favour of protecting the consumer against harmful products, whereas Lord Buckmaster's concern was to protect commercial concerns from litigation. In the end of course, Lord Atkin's view prevailed. Policy considerations play an integral part in decisions to recognise or deny a duty of care in circumstances where there is no precedent directly in point.

The scope of the duty: in respect of what is a duty owed?

2–04   Lord Atkin appears to have spoken of injury in fairly general terms. It is clear, however, that, just as duties are only owed to individuals or defined classes of person, they are also owed only in respect of particular types of harm and do not necessarily cover every consequence of the defender's conduct. This point has become increasingly important over time as duties of care have been recognised in a growing range of circumstances and the concern to keep liability for negligence within bounds has been more keenly felt as a consequence.

The general rule was clarified by the House of Lords in another Scottish appeal, *Muir v Glasgow Corporation*. Participants in a Sunday school picnic in King's Park, Glasgow, sought shelter from the rain in a tea-room run by the defenders. The corporation's employee on the premises, Mrs Alexander, gave permission for the picnic to be brought indoors and allowed an urn full of boiling water to be carried down a passageway to the tea-room. One of the two persons carrying the urn dropped his handle and several children who were queuing to buy sweets were scalded by the spillage. It was held that the spillage was not foreseeable as a reasonable and probable consequence of Mrs Alexander's conduct in allowing the urn to be carried. She was entitled to assume that the carriers would have been reasonably careful. As Lord Thankerton explained, "it has long been held in Scotland that all that a person can be bound to foresee are the reasonable and probable consequences of the failure to take care, judged by the standard of the ordinary reasonable man". The same point was made by Lord MacMillan: "Legal liability is limited to those consequences of our acts which a reasonable man of ordinary intelligence and experience so acting would have in contemplation."

It follows then, that if A, acting as a reasonable person, ought to foresee a risk of damage to B's property as a probable consequence of A's conduct, then if A does not take the care of a reasonable person in performing his operations he will be liable for any property harm caused to B. If A's actions cause personal injury to B in circumstances where personal injury would not have been foreseeable to a reasonable person in A's position, then there is no liability for that, because no duty arose in respect of personal injury. An example would be burning garden refuse on a windy day close to a neighbour's fence. The spread of fire to the neighbour's garden and destruction of the fence are foreseeable consequences if the fire is not contained. Unless he or she is known to take naps in their shrubbery, the immolation of the neighbour is not. Of course, in practice, personal injury and property harm are foreseeable consequences of conduct that often go together. If A drives carelessly it is foreseeable that A may both damage another vehicle and injure or kill its occupants. If A knocks down a pedestrian breaking his or her legs, then A cannot argue that they should not also be liable for the replacement of the Armani suit the pedestrian was wearing at the time. Personal injury and property damage are, however, forms of loss for which duties of care are readily recognised provided, of course that such harm is foreseeable. Determining the scope of a duty becomes a more critical business in the context of other forms of loss in which a more restrictive approach is taken. So, for example, in the context of pure economic loss (where the only loss suffered is financial), in *Caparo Industries Plc v Dickman* a firm of auditors conducted an audit of a company negligently so as to show the company in profit when it was in fact in deficit. Although auditors owe a statutory duty to shareholders as members of the company, it was determined that no duty was owed to certain specific shareholders in respect of the losses they incurred when they mounted a takeover bid proceeding on the basis of the incorrect financial information provided in the audit. The auditors were not bound to have anticipated this particular consequence of their action. The case of *Caparo* is also significant for its emphasis on proximity that plays a role not only in identifying the persons who ought to be within the contemplation of the defender, but clearly extends also to the question of whether specific losses would have been foreseeable to defenders and therefore fall within the scope of the duty.

Duty of care: remote risks

2–05 There is some conceptual overlap between the scope of duty and breach of duty when it is considered whether a particular harmful occurrence is something against which precautions ought to have been put in place. This question tends to arise in the context of remote risks. Drawing a line between on the one hand, risks that have as their reasonable and probable consequence harm to others (and in respect of which therefore a duty arises) and on the other, those that are present, but not very likely to materialise is not an exact science. Moreover, the process is complicated by the fact that the question can be addressed in terms of whether a given risk falls within the scope of the duty or, alternatively, accepting that a duty is owed, analysis may proceed on the basis of whether the duty has been breached. It may seem contradictory to state on one hand that duties only arise in respect of harm that is the reasonable and probable consequence of conduct, but to proceed on the basis that a duty was in place and consider whether it was breached in respect of some particular consequence, but in practice conduct may give rise to a number of different risks, some of which are more likely to materialise than others. *Muir v Glasgow Corporation* provides an example. The defenders were in fact under a common law duty of care as occupiers of premises towards those entering the premises. Was it the case that the granting of permission to carry the tea urn fell outwith the scope of the duty because this carried no risk of probable harm or is the decision better explained by reference to the point that a duty requires only that reasonable care be taken and that the granting of permission was not unreasonable given the lack of a foreseeable risk and so there was no breach? The answer is not immediately obvious. The modern tendency in pleadings appears to be to focus on the scope of the duty: the pursuer must contend that they were owed a duty in respect of the particular type of harm of which they are complaining. As Lord Bridge stated in *Caparo Industries Plc v Dickman*: "It is never sufficient to ask simply whether A owes B a duty of care. It is always necessary to determine the scope of the duty by reference to the kind of damage from which A must take care to save B."

Observations on liability for remote risks can be seen in this dictum of Lord Oaksey:

> "The standard of care in the law of negligence is the standard of an ordinary careful man, but in my opinion an ordinary careful man does not take precautions against every foreseeable risk. He can, of course, foresee the possibility of many risks, but life would be almost impossible if he were to attempt to take precautions against every risk which he can foresee. He takes precautions against risks which are reasonably likely to happen. Many foreseeable risks are extremely unlikely to happen and cannot be guarded against except by almost complete isolation."

The context for these remarks was the English House of Lords case of *Bolton v Stone*. In that case a cricket ball was struck right out of a cricket ground where it injured a person around 100 yards from the wicket. While the event was foreseeable, balls had been struck out of the ground six times in the previous 30 years, the defendants who operated the cricket ground were not obliged to have guarded against it. The risk of injury was so remote that a reasonable person would not have anticipated it. *Bolton v Stone* may be contrasted with the case of *Lamond v Glasgow Corporation* in which a golf ball was hit onto a footpath where it struck the pursuer on the head. In that case the duty of care was breached since the event was not only possible, but also probable. It was established in evidence that on average 6,000 golf balls were played onto the footpath every year, although there was no previously reported instance of anybody having been struck.

Care must be taken with the view that risks that are foreseeable, but improbable, may be ignored. In reference to *Bolton*, Lord Reid, in *Overseas Tankship (UK) Ltd v The Miller Steamship Co Pty Ltd (The Wagon Mound (No.2))*, explained that there must be some valid reason for ignoring the risk, for example the expense or inconvenience of guarding against the risk. The question is whether a reasonable person, careful of the safety of their neighbour, would think it right to neglect the risk. Certainly, as Lord Oaksey suggested, the law cannot seek the elimination of all risk taking. That would be an unwarrantable inhibition on activity.

Duty of care: unpredictable consequences
The House of Lords decision in *Hughes v Lord Advocate* demonstrates a 2–06
very important point. Although the precise way in which an accident occurs may not be reasonably foreseeable, if some accident of that type or general nature is foreseeable then liability may be established. This case involved a hole in the road, covered with a tent, but otherwise insufficiently guarded. Boys investigated with a paraffin lamp that had been marking the road works. The lamp was knocked down the hole, the paraffin vaporised and ignited causing an explosion that burned one of the boys badly. It was held that the explosion was not foreseeable. However, it was foreseeable that a child might enter the tent with a lamp, that paraffin might spill and that the child might be burned. Accordingly, liability was established.

Similarly, in *Wilson v Chief Constable of Lothian and Borders Police* a man died of hypothermia having been released in a drunken condition by police at an isolated place at 05.45 on a January morning. It had been snowing heavily, the temperature was 0°C. The body was found a week later over two miles from the site of release. It was held that the police were not bound to have foreseen the man's death from hypothermia, but they should have foreseen that he would be exposed to various risks of severe harm. They were under a particular duty to have regard to the reasonably foreseeable consequences of his release. The officers concerned had failed to direct their minds to the likely consequences of their act and had exposed the deceased to unnecessary risk. The chain of events that was foreseeable was not different in kind from those that led to his death.

The rule, that one is only liable for foreseeable consequences, is subject to an exception in personal injury cases. Here, the defender takes their victim as they find them. Thus, in *McKillen v Barclay-Curle*, the negligent defender who was liable for the pursuer's fractured rib was also liable for the consequent reactivation of the pursuer's tuberculosis, even though this could not have been foreseen by the defender.

BREACH OF DUTY

Breach of duty and the standard of care

2–07 Establishing a duty of care is only the first step in an action based on negligence. Next it has to be established that the duty was breached. In determining breach, the defender's conduct is measured against the standard of care. The standard of care means the level of care that must be taken in the course of observing the duty. In short, it serves to give content to the abstract notion of duty of care. The standard of care addresses the question: how much care should be taken? Negligence consists in a failure to meet the standard of care. To incur liability, the defender's conduct must be shown to have been negligent.

The level of care that should be taken if the duty of care is to be fulfilled is that of a reasonable person in the circumstances of the defender. Thus, the defender must exercise the level of care of a reasonably careful plumber, a reasonable electrician, a reasonable structural engineer, a reasonable neurosurgeon or a reasonable car park attendant, depending on the context. The standard of care then is objective. In *Harris v Perry* the Court of Appeal overturned a finding by the trial judge that a woman was negligent in failing to supervise properly children of different ages playing on a bouncy castle. A larger boy broke the skull of an 11-year-old when attempting a summersault while the woman's back was turned. The standard of care applicable was that which a reasonably careful parent would have shown towards her own children. There was no breach of duty in this case. Children cannot be watched 100 per cent of the time. The level of care required does not vary with the individual idiosyncrasies or propensities of the defender. In *Nettleship v Weston* it was held that a learner driver owes the same standard of care to other road users as an experienced driver. If this seems harsh on the learner driver, the point is that other road users and pedestrians are entitled to expect a certain degree of care, not differing standards according to the experience or lack of it of the driver.

While the standard is always that of the reasonable person in the circumstances, the circumstances themselves affect the level of care required. As Lord MacMillan stated in *Muir v Glasgow Corporation*, "there is no absolute standard, but it may be said generally that the degree of care required varies directly with the risk involved". The same point was expressed in *Mackintosh v Mackintosh* by Lord Neaves, "no prudent man in carrying a lighted candle through a powder magazine would fail to take more care than if he was going through a damp cellar".

It is for the pursuer to establish the standard of care by specification in pleadings of the measures that ought to have been taken. This gives the defender notice of the case against him without which the pursuers pleadings will be challenged as irrelevant and lacking in specification. A challenge to relevancy is made on the basis that even if the pursuer succeeds in proving all the facts that they have averred, they are not entitled in law to the remedy they seek. A successful challenge to relevancy will result in dismissal of the case, but this only occurs where it is clear to the court that the action is bound to fail. A more common result in delictual actions is for the case to be set down for proof before answer. This means that the court will not reach a decision on the merits of the action until evidence has been led at proof and the facts established. Actions that reach this stage in litigation will normally be settled before proof actually takes place. Indeed, many case reports in delict, including *Donoghue v Stevenson*, are actually concerned, not with determining liability as such, but with the question of whether the pursuer has established a relevant case.

The standard of care will vary according to the level of risk and potential degree of harm should the risk materialise. Broadly, the highest standard of care will apply to high risk activities that will cause much destruction or death if things go wrong. The lowest standard of care will apply where the risk of harm is small and any injury or damage will be relatively minor. The standard of care will lie somewhere between these two extremes when there is a lower risk with potentially severe consequences or a high risk with lesser consequences, but the standard can never exceed what is reasonable in the circumstances. This means that it is also relevant to consider the practicability, expense and disadvantage to the defender of taking the precautions contended for by the pursuer. This approach to determining the appropriate standard of care is termed "the calculus of risk" and derives from the judgment of Lord Reid in *Morris v West Hartlepool Steam Navigation Co Ltd*. There is a duty on employers to weigh on the one hand, the magnitude of risk, the likelihood of an accident happening and the possible gravity of any accident against, on the other hand, the difficulty, expense and disadvantage of taking any particular precaution. While the calculus of risk is commonly illustrated by reference to employment cases, the basic approach is not restricted to the employment field.

In *Brisco v Secretary of State for Scotland* a prison officer sought damages of £2,000 in respect of a broken bone in his little toe, sustained when a heavy fence post thrown from above landed on him during a simulated riot. The pursuer contended that his employers were in breach of their duty to him in failing to issue an instruction forbidding the throwing of heavy objects. Given the need for riot training of prison officers under realistic circumstances, such an instruction would have amounted to a disadvantage. This disadvantage was sufficient to outweigh the relatively slight risk involved. The standard of care contended for by the pursuer could not be upheld and there was therefore no breach of duty.

In *Latimer v AEC Ltd* a factory floor became slippery after flooding. Three tons of sawdust was put down on the floor, but the plaintiff slipped on an uncovered part of the floor and was injured. He argued that the factory should have been closed down. The House of Lords held that the employer had done all that a reasonable employer would have done. Closing down the factory would have meant a loss of production, and the expense and disadvantage of this was not outweighed by the relatively small danger to which the plaintiff had been exposed. Latimer may be contrasted with *Collins v First Quench Retailing Ltd.* In this case the manager of an off-license store suffered depression and post-traumatic stress disorder following an armed robbery, the risk of which was foreseeable in that shop. Her contention that her employers should have provided security screens was not accepted by the court, but the precautions taken were otherwise found to be inadequate. The employer was negligent specifically in requiring the pursuer to work on her own. It may be noted that the pursuer's loss was recognisable psychiatric harm and therefore a reparable personal injury. Lesser conditions, such as anxiety, are not generally recoverable in negligence.

There are other related factors that may be brought to bear on determining the standard of care in appropriate circumstances. Known characteristics of the pursuer that make them especially vulnerable to risks may serve to raise the standard applicable. In *Paris v Stepney Borough Council* the claimant, who had lost one eye in the war, was employed as a fitter. While attempting to remove a bolt with a hammer, a chip of metal entered his good eye and he was rendered completely blind. This would have been prevented had goggles been supplied. At the time it was not standard practice to provide fitters with such protection, but, nevertheless, his employers were held in breach of duty. In this case, while the risk of injury may have been no different from other fitters, the potential consequences of an injury were very much greater. The standard of care was accordingly set higher than normal; specifically, an employer acting reasonably would have provided eye-protection. A more recent example is found in *St George v Home Office*. Prison authorities were found negligent in allocating a top bunk to a prisoner known to suffer epileptic seizures on withdrawal from alcohol and heroin.

Normal practice then is not always a reliable guide to the standard of care. The House of Lords decision in *Brown v Rolls Royce* demonstrates that failure to adopt a normal practice is not conclusive proof of negligence, but merely a fact from which negligence may be inferred. The plaintiff contracted dermatitis. He was a machine oiler whose hands were constantly in contact with oil. Evidence was led to show that it was common practice for employers to provide Rozalex #1, a barrier cream. Rolls Royce had not done so, but they had sought medical advice on the issue and contended that Rozalex was not an effective prophylactic. They had made alternative provision in the form of adequate washing facilities. Rolls Royce was not in breach. They had not neglected to take precautions, but had considered the issue, made provision and had demonstrated the conduct and judgment of a reasonable employer. Thus, normal practice may be of evidential value, but will not, in itself, determine the issue.

Finally, the utility of conduct may justify exposing others to risks which would be negligent in other circumstances. The standard of care required of a police driver responding to a call may be lower than that incumbent on the ordinary driver in normal circumstances (*Gilfillan v Barbour*). In *Daborn v Bath Tramways Motor Co Ltd* the utility of having American-built, left-hand drive ambulances in wartime was such as to justify the increased risk from the use of a vehicle with restricted rear view and an inability to signal. Having put a warning notice on the back of the vehicle, the driver was not negligent when she turned right and collided with a bus that was overtaking. Lord Denning took the view in *Watt v Hertfordshire County Council* that, "you must balance the risk against the end to be achieved". In that case a fireman was injured by a heavy-lifting jack mounted on a lorry that was not adapted to that purpose. In fact, the jack was very rarely used, the lorry that was adapted for it was out on another call, the lorry used was the only vehicle present that could carry the jack, the firemen were on their way to rescue a woman stuck under a heavy vehicle within a very short distance of the fire station and calling out the next nearest fire station would have caused a significant delay when assistance was urgently required. Since the view was taken that the risk to the woman's life outweighed the risk in using the lorry, the Court of Appeal rejected the fireman's claim. While reluctance to characterise the action of the fire brigade in this case as negligent is understandable, it is arguably unfortunate that the claimant was denied compensation in the circumstances.

CAUSATION

Where a duty of care has been recognised and where the defender's breach **2–08** of duty is established, it then falls to the pursuer to show that the loss complained of is attributable to the breach. Causation must be proved on a balance of probabilities. Causation is required for intentional wrongdoing also, but in such cases, it is less likely to be contentious. In cases where harm follows immediately and directly from the defender's negligence— or other form of wrongful conduct—causation is generally straightforward. Causation is more likely to become an issue in cases where harm is not immediate, but follows a sequence of events.

There are two requirements for causation. First, the breach must be the factual cause of the harm. This is termed the *causa sine qua non*. Second, the breach must also be the legal cause of the harm. This is termed the *causa causans*. Unless the breach is both the factual and legal cause, causation will not be established and the action will fail accordingly. If driver A becomes distracted, mounts the pavement and kills pedestrian B on the spot, then the factual and legal causes of B's death are indistinguishable and causation is clear. A would be liable for B's death, which is entirely attributable to A's breach of duty. Where, on the other hand A does not kill B, but breaks his legs and, while recovering in hospital, B contracts an MRSA infection (Methicillin-resistant Staphylococcus aureus) and dies from that, A would remain liable for personal injury to B, but would not be liable for B's death. This is despite the fact that A's breach is the factual cause of B's death since we can say, "but for A's negligence B would not have died" (as he would not have been in the position to contract MRSA). Factual causation is a necessary, but not sufficient condition to establish liability. In this example A's negligence is the *causa sine qua non* of B's death, but it is not the *causa causans*, that is the immediate, effective or dominant cause. The *causa causans*, or legal cause, of B's death is the MRSA for which A cannot be held responsible. The MRSA operates here as a *novus actus interveniens* breaking the chain of causation linking A's breach to B's death.

A *novus actus interveniens* means "new act intervening". It is important to note that an event coming between the breach and the ultimate injury or loss will not break the chain of causation if it is a foreseeable consequence of the breach. If A pulls out of a junction without checking that the road is clear, causing B to swerve to avoid a collision, and B knocks C off her motorbike, then A's breach is both the factual and legal cause of injury to C and damage to her bike. B's action is not a *novus actus interveniens* breaking the chain of causation. B's action in swerving is entirely attributable to A's breach and is, moreover, not a wrongful act. A and not B will be liable to C. As Lord Wright expressed it in *The Oropesa*:

> "To break the chain of causation it must be shown that there is something which I will call ultroneous, something unwarrantable, a new cause which disturbs the sequence of events, something which can be described as either unreasonable or extraneous or extrinsic. I doubt whether the law can be stated more precisely than that."

In *Fraser v Bell* a ferocious dog jumped on a coalman who dropped his sack of coal on the foot of another man. The man responsible for the dog was liable for the injured foot. Dropping the sack was an involuntary act, the natural consequence of the attack and not a *novus actus interveniens* breaking the chain of causation. Similarly, in *Scott v Shepherd* a person who threw a lighted firework into a crowd was liable for the injuries it caused even though two persons had picked it up and acting for their own safety, had thrown it on before it finally exploded. The acts of throwing the firework on were probable consequences of the original act.

In *McKew v Holland & Hannon & Cubitts (Scotland) Ltd* the pursuer injured his ankle as a result of the defenders' negligence. His leg thereafter was liable to "give way" on occasions. After the accident he went to visit a flat. Access to the flat was by way of a stair with no handrail. The pursuer descended the stairway without care, his leg gave way, he panicked and jumped down 10 steps causing injury to his other leg. The court held the defenders liable for the original injury, but not the second. By descending the stairs without care the pursuer's own act constituted a *novus actus interveniens*. His behaviour was unreasonable. The defenders' breach was the *causa sine qua non* of the second injury, but it was not the *causa causans*.

Of course, some cases fail because pursuers fail to establish that the breach complained of was the factual cause of the harm. In *McWilliams v Sir William Arrol & Co* employers were in breach of their duty since they failed to provide a steel erector (scaffolder) with a safety belt. The defenders were not, however, liable when he plunged to his death since it was established in evidence that, had he been given a belt, the steel erector would not have worn it. It could not be said that "but for" the defenders' breach the pursuer would not have been injured. Similarly, in *McKinlay v British Steel Corporation* the pursuer claimed that he had not been instructed and encouraged to wear safety goggles in accordance with the duty on the defenders. On the evidence it was held that the pursuer had failed to establish that he would have worn goggles if instructed to do so. The defenders were assoilzied. In *Barnett v Chelsea and Kensington Hospital Management Committee* the casualty officer was in breach of duty in failing to see a patient who presented during the night with violent vomiting. The patient died later of arsenic poisoning. The hospital was not liable despite the breach, because it was established that the patient would have died anyway. His death was not attributable to the doctor's breach of duty, but to poisoning. In *McTear v Imperial Tobacco Company Ltd* the pursuer failed to establish that her husband would not have got lung cancer "but for" smoking John Player cigarettes. The defenders' contention, that the deceased would have continued to smoke and would have got lung cancer anyway even without the availability of their own brands, prevailed.

Multiple source causation

It is not always possible to attribute an injury or illness to a single source. **2–09** Of course, where all sources of the harm arise from breaches by the same defender the defender will be fully liable. Difficulties arise when it is impossible to determine which source caused the harm, especially where some sources do not involve negligence. In *Wardlaw v Bonnington Castings* the pursuer contracted pneumoconiosis from breathing in dust at work. The dust might have come from the hammer that he operated, for which there was no known means of providing protection and therefore no breach of duty on the part of the employers. Equally the dust might have come from grinders and other machinery for which protection could have been, but was not, provided. Accordingly, the employers were not in breach in respect of one possible source, but were in breach in respect of the other. The House of Lords held that the pursuer could succeed in negligence if he could show that dust from the source for which the defenders were in breach had materially contributed to his injuries. In this case the "but for" test was relaxed. A further development took place in *McGhee v National Coal Board*. In that case also there were two possible sources of harm, one of which involved breach of duty and the other did not. The pursuer worked in a kiln and was exposed to dust. There was no means of effecting protection and therefore no breach of duty. The other potential source was the failure of the defenders to supply washing facilities in breach of duty. This meant that the pursuer cycled home from work every day in a generally dusty condition. Again, it was impossible to determine whether it was the exposure to dust or the lack of washing facilities that was the effective cause of the pursuer's dermatitis. The pursuer may have contracted dermatitis purely through his work or it might have been that there would have been no harm had he been able to clean up before going home. In this case the House of Lords relaxed the "but for" test and held that the pursuer could succeed if the breach had materially contributed to the *risk* of harm.

Further difficulties arise when the sources of harm originate with different defenders. It would be fair to describe this aspect of the law as complicated. *Fairchild v Glenhaven Funeral Services* involved a number of conjoined cases. The question before the House of Lords was whether claimants, exposed to asbestos fibres by different employers over different periods, should be able to recover damages in respect of resultant mesothelioma. The problem for pursuers in such cases is that the "but for" test, that is factual causation, cannot be established on the balance of probabilities and, whereas in *Wardlaw* and *McGhee*, it could at least be said that source of harm originated with the defender, to find liability in the circumstances that presented in *Fairchild* is to run the risk of imposing liability on a party with no role in the eventual harm. The view was taken in the House of Lords that this risk was outweighed by the risk of denying compensation to those suffering from what has been aptly described as a hideous illness. Drawing on *McGhee* and in view of the fact that the risk of mesothelioma increases with total exposure to asbestos, the "but for" test was relaxed again and proof, on a balance of probabilities that the defender had materially increased the *risk* of illness, was sufficient to establish liability. Where this was established against more than one defender liability was held to be joint and several.

Subsequently, in the House of Lords case of *Barker v Corus* liability was held to be proportionate between the defenders, that is divisible in proportion to the magnitude of the risk of injury to which each had exposed the claimant. The claimant had been exposed to three sources of asbestos at different times. For one of these he was himself responsible as he was self-employed at the time. Parliament responded promptly to this decision in enacting s.3 of the Compensation Act 2006. This provision applies only in mesothelioma cases. It reinstates joint and several liability where defenders have been found liable for exposure to asbestos while reserving the possibility of a reduction in damages for contributory negligence. While each responsible defender is jointly and severally liable to the claimant, the respective contributions made by the different defenders between themselves may vary. Section 3(4) provides that apportionment between defenders may be imposed by the court or may be agreed between the defenders. These rules apply once the court has determined the question of liability. It was made clear in the later case of *Sienkiewicz v Grief* that determining liability remains a matter for the common law. *Sienkiewicz v Greif* is also notable for holding that the *Fairchild/ Barker* exception to the normal rule of causation—that is, liability established on the basis of a material increase in *risk*—applies equally in cases where there is a single defender. *Sienkiewicz* involved two conjoined cases: one potential source of contact with asbestos was through past employers, the defendants; the other potential source was environmental for which nobody could be held liable. Despite having made a proportionately small increase to the risk of harm, this was still regarded as material and the liability of the defendants was upheld in the Supreme Court.

In cases in which the *Fairchild/Barker* exception applies but the Compensation Act does not, then liability remains proportionate according to the degree of risk created following *Barker*. This was affirmed by the Supreme Court in *International Energy Ltd v Zurich Insurance Plc*. The exception applies where it is clear that a delict has occurred, but attribution is scientifically impossible. The Compensation Act will not apply where the harm is not mesothelioma, but the *Fairchild/Barker* exception is not restricted to mesothelioma cases as demonstrated in the case of *Heneghan v Manchester Dry Docks Ltd* which involved lung cancer. The *International Energy* case fell to be determined under the common law, because the action was first raised in the Royal Court in Guernsey to which the statute did not extend.

Finally, there is now a statutory compensation scheme in the form of the Mesothelioma Act 2014 and associated secondary legislation. The scheme provides compensation for victims of mesothelioma and eligible dependants of those who have died from this illness in circumstances where the responsible employer or insurer can no longer be found, usually because they are no longer in existence. Given the lengthy period between contamination by asbestos fibres and the onset of mesothelioma, some 30 to 40 years, such circumstances are by no means unusual.

REMOTENESS

There may be no end to the consequences of negligent conduct. The **2–10** concept of remoteness operates to draw a line between losses that must be compensated and those that the victim must bear. Damages will not be awarded in respect of losses that are too remote. It is common to cite a dictum of Lord Kinloch in *Allan v Barclay*:

> "The grand rule on the subject of damages is that none can be claimed except such as naturally and directly arise out of the wrong done; and such therefore, as may reasonably be supposed to have been in the view of the wrongdoer."

This conflates direct consequences with those that are reasonably foreseeable, an issue which has caused some difficulty in English law. Lord Rodger settled any ambiguity, for Scots law anyway, in the House of Lords in *Simmons v British Steel Plc*.

"Once liability is established in terms of duty and breach the starting point is that the defender is not to be held liable for consequences that are not reasonably foreseeable."

Questions of remoteness are not entirely distinct from questions of duty or causation. Certainly, the defender will not be called to answer for harm that is not within the scope of the duty and there will be no liability even for foreseeable harm where there has been a break in the causal chain. Remoteness can be viewed as dealing with the consequential losses that flow less immediately from the incident. Those that are foreseeable will be compensated, speculative losses will not. A day spent in hospital might mean a missed job interview and the consequences that follow from that could include penury, alcoholism, marital break-up and homelessness, but these could not reasonably be within the foresight of the party who caused the injury. A speculative loss might be the chance of a prize at the local flower show when the dahlia bed has been dug up by the neighbour's dog, but there is no guarantee that the destroyed blooms would have won. Loss of a chance may be reparable, but only within narrowly defined circumstances. In *Kyle v P&J Stormonth-Darling WS* a firm of solicitors was held liable in damages to its client for failing to lodge appeal papers. It was by no means certain that the client would have won the appeal, but loss in such circumstances can be seen in terms of the loss of a legal right. This is similar in principle to the earlier English case of *Kitchen v Royal Air Force*. In *Gregg v Scott* the House of Lords by a majority rejected a claim based on reduced chances of recovery from cancer where treatment had been delayed because of an earlier misdiagnosis. The delay reduced this chance from 42 per cent to 25 per cent, so even without misdiagnosis the claimant always had a less than evens chance.

3. NEGLIGENCE II: SPECIAL CASES

Introduction

Chapter 2 covered generally applicable principles of liability for **3–01**
negligence. This chapter covers circumstances in which there are additional
or "special" considerations. What makes a case "special" so that it requires
consideration here? The question of duty may arise in novel circumstances,
that is in circumstances for which there is no governing precedent or where
precedent is against the pursuer. In such cases the pursuer has the task of
persuading the court that, in the circumstances, a duty of care ought to be
recognised. As Lord MacMillan famously stated, "the categories of
negligence are never closed". Courts have extended the coverage of duties
of care in some significant ways over the years, but have generally been
wary of opening the floodgates to an overwhelming volume of litigation.
Expansions of the law tend to be constrained within narrow margins. This
means that for some forms of loss or in some circumstances liability may
depend on rules which are not of general application.

The topics to be covered are: liability for pure economic loss; liability
for the acts of third parties; and liability for nervous shock. These topics
have all arisen from the recognition of duties of care in novel
circumstances. The relationship between common law and duties imposed
by statute needs to be understood and this will precede coverage of the
liability of public bodies. It must be stated at the outset that cases do not
always fit nicely into categories and so, for example, much of the case law
covered under liability for third parties will involve public body defenders.
The chapter concludes with the current approach taken to the recognition
of duties in novel circumstances.

ECONOMIC LOSS

Economic or financial losses fall into three types: derivative, secondary **3–02**
and pure. Derivative economic losses are the financial losses that may
follow from any delict, the cost of replacing a car or loss of earnings and
so on. These losses form the patrimonial part of any claim for damages.
Secondary economic losses are incurred when negligently caused harm to
one party leads to financial loss for another. Such losses are not recoverable
in delict from the negligent party, because the duty of care owed to the first
victim will not usually extend to the second also. Secondary losses are too
remote. In *Reavis v Clan Line Steamers* the pursuer failed to recover sums
lost from performances she was contracted to provide, but could not,
because members of her orchestra had drowned due to the negligence of the
defenders. In *Dynamco v Holland*, Hannen & Cubitts financial losses from
factory downtime were incurred when an employee of the defenders
severed the power supply while working with a digger. Since the power

line was the property of the electricity company, the pursuers' losses were secondary and not recoverable.

Pure economic loss arises where only financial harm is suffered. That is financial harm unaccompanied by any injury or property damage or harm to reputation and so on. Pure economic losses are recoverable in the intentional delicts. They are also recoverable in contract. Historically, such losses were not recoverable in negligence. While *Donoghue v Stephenson* had been applied in cases of personal injury and property damage more or less generally, no duty of care to guard against purely financial harm was recognised before 1966. The principle, that a party could recover damages when loss was incurred as a result of reliance on the accuracy of a statement provided by another, in circumstances where this reliance was reasonable and the party making the statement knew or ought to have known that the recipient was relying on him, was established by the House of Lords in *Hedley-Byrne v Heller and Partners*. In that case an advertising agency (Hedley-Byrne) had sought the assurance of a client's bankers (Heller and Partners) that the client was in a financial position to pay for work instructed. Having received a positive assurance, an extensive advertising campaign was launched, the client went into liquidation and the agency was left out of pocket to the tune of £17,661.18/10d. While the possibility of recovery of losses was recognised in principle, the fact that the bankers had explicitly made their statement "without responsibility" meant that Hedley-Byrne did not succeed. In these circumstances, the defendants could hardly have been said to have assumed responsibility. It may be noted that disclaimers such as this would now be subject to a statutory test of fairness under s.16(1)(b) of the Unfair Contract Terms Act 1977 or s.62 of the Consumer Rights Act 2015 where either is applicable.

Hedley-Byrne has provided a foundation for the law on negligent misstatement that has been employed in a variety of contexts, notably where house purchasers have lost money having acted in reliance on negligently conducted property surveys (see e.g. *Martin v Bell-Ingram*; *Smith v Eric S Bush*; *Bank of Scotland v Fuller-Peiser*). Note that surveyors may now be liable for losses to purchasers under the "single survey" scheme introduced by the Housing (Scotland) Act 2006. The law on negligent misstatement was reviewed by the House of Lords in 1990 in *Caparo Industries Plc v Dickman*. In *Caparo* shareholders relied on a negligently conducted audit when they purchased a majority shareholding in a company. No duty was owed by the auditors who could not have been expected to know that the overly optimistic figures given in the audit would have been relied on either by the shareholders in question or for this purpose. The loss was not foreseeable and proximity between the parties was lacking.

The principles underlying recovery for negligent misstatement have been extended to cover the negligent provision of professional services more generally. In *Henderson v Merrett Syndicates* it was held in the House of Lords that the relationship between members of Lloyd's syndicates and underwriting agents disclosed an assumption of responsibility by the defendant to the plaintiff with concomitant reliance by the plaintiff on the quality of services provided, leading to liability when loss resulted from the negligent delivery of those services. A duty of care in delict was recognised independent of contractual relations between the parties. Under *Henderson* rules, a duty of care will arise when there has been a voluntary assumption of responsibility by the defender for the economic interests of the pursuer. The assumption of responsibility need not be express, it may be inferred (see e.g. *Smith v Eric S Bush*; *Royal Bank of Scotland v Bannerman, Johnstone, Maclay*). The pursuer must have relied on the defender's exercise of skill and expertise and the defender must know that the pursuer is so relying. A disclaimer will negate a duty, but it will be subject to the statutory test as noted above. In *Cramasco LLP v Ogilvie-Grant* a party who induced another to enter into a contact of lease for a grousemoor was held to have assumed responsibility for the accuracy of his figures when he misrepresented the number of birds available to be shot.

LIABILITY FOR THE CRIMINAL ACTS OF THIRD PARTIES

Other than in cases where liability is vicarious, parties cannot normally be **3–03** called upon to answer for the acts of other people. The maxim is *culpa tenet suos auctores* (fault attaches to its authors). The act of an independent third party will, in most cases, break any causal link between the defender and victim. In *Dorset Yacht Co v Home Office* borstal boys (young offenders) on an island in Poole harbour sought to escape by commandeering a yacht. The defendants were held liable in the House of Lords for the damage done to the yacht, which suffered a collision under the poor seamanship of the escapees. The boys were under the supervision of prison officers. These officers were negligent in having left the boys unsupervised. The event was foreseeable, the boys had records of absconding and were likely to cause damage if they did so. The predictability of the boys' actions consequent on the negligence of the officers left the principles of causation intact, but the decision raised the prospect of delictual liability for the criminal acts of third parties for the first time. In *Maloco v Littlewoods* the owners of an empty cinema, the Regal in Dunfermline, were not liable for damage to neighbouring property caused by children breaking into the cinema and starting fires that then spread. It was determined in the House of Lords that the owners of property did not owe a duty to neighbours to secure their own premises against entry. The element of control over the wrongdoers critical to the decision in *Dorset Yacht Co* was missing from *Maloco*, but the decision went against Scottish authorities (*Evans v Glasgow District Council*; *Squires v Perth & Kinross District Council*) in which duties in analogous circumstances had indeed been recognised. The decisions in these cases had been based on the foreseeability of the consequences of leaving property unsecured. In *Maloco* a Scottish judge, Lord McKay, viewed the events in that case as unforeseeable, but the decision is probably better explained as following the English Court of Appeal case of *Perl*

Exporters v Camden LBC. Despite having been put on notice of the danger of thieves gaining access to the claimants' premises through derelict property in the control of the defendants, no duty was owed when this transpired. Lord Goff stated:

> "Is every occupier of a terraced house under a duty to his neighbours to shut his windows or lock his door when he goes out, or to keep access to his cellars secure, or even to remove his fire escape, at the risk of being held liable in damages if thieves thereby obtain access to his own house and thence to his neighbour's house? I cannot think that the law imposes any such duty."

Clearly Lord Goff had the broader effects of the decision in mind, but the approach demonstrates reluctance to impose liability for pure omissions. Arguably, in the past Scots law has been less exercised by this particular consideration, but the extent to which this remains the case is moot. An argument along these lines met with no success in *Mitchell v Glasgow City Council*. Mitchell was a council tenant who had had problems with a neighbour, Drummond, over some six years. Drummond was noisy, threatening and violent and unpleasant incidents occurred on a regular basis. Following a meeting with the council in which Drummond was threatened with eviction he killed Mitchell with an iron bar. Mitchell's widow and daughter contended that the council was negligent in failing to warn Mitchell of the meeting, but it was held in the House of Lords, applying *Maloco*, that no such duty was owed. In *Thomson v Scottish Ministers* a prisoner on release murdered a woman. The lack of proximity between the responsible authorities and the victim meant that no duty was owed her. The case is similar in principle to *Hill v Chief Constable of West Yorkshire*. By contrast, when a prisoner, known to the authorities to pose a serious risk to another prisoner attempted to murder him, *Dorset Yacht Co* was applied and the victim succeeded in his claim (*Kaizer v Scottish Ministers*).

In *Michael v Chief Constable of South Wales* a woman made an emergency call to police reporting that her former partner had assaulted her and was about to return having threatened to kill her. There was negligence in the process of handling the call and it was down-graded from requiring an immediate response. In a second call the woman was heard to scream. Police officers attended 15 minutes after the second call by which time the caller had been stabbed 70 times and was dead. The Supreme Court held by a 3:2 majority, Lord Kerr and Lady Hale dissenting, that no duty was owed by the police. Certainly, the culprit was not in the control of the police. The arguments in the case are complicated, but one factor of some significance was that the call handler had said nothing to the caller to amount to an assumption of responsibility or to induce reliance. Lord Kerr observed in his dissenting speech:

"That the incidence of liability should depend on the happenstance of the telephonist uttering words that can be construed as conveying an unmistakable undertaking that the police will prevent the feared attack is surely unacceptable."

In the view of Lord Kerr in the circumstances of the case, where the police knew of an imminent threat to the life of an identified person that they had the ability to prevent without danger to themselves, proximity could be established. It may be noted that more recently the police, having failed to respond adequately to a 999 call made by her mother, have been held to owe a duty of care to a woman who took her own life (*Sherratt v Chief Constable of Greater Manchester Police*). In *Rathband v Chief Constable of Northumbria* there was no liability to a police officer who was shot and blinded by a man who had phoned the police threatening to shoot officers. The claimant argued that he should have been warned of the threat, but the incident occurred within eight minutes of the threat being issued at which time the cell-site analysis had not been completed and the source not located, it was too early for the risk to the claimant in particular to have been identified and there was no negligence.

In conclusion, a duty of care in respect of the criminal acts of third parties may be recognised when the defender is in the position to exercise control over the third party and avoid foreseeable risks. Equally, there will be a duty where the defender has assumed responsibility for the interests of the victim. On the question of whether a duty arises when an emergency call is made, *Michael*, as a Supreme Court decision is the current governing authority, but it also has to be seen in the more general context of the civil liability of the police, a matter considered in detail in *Robinson v Chief Constable of West Yorkshire*.

NERVOUS SHOCK

The subject matter of this section concerns liability for nervous shock. This **3–04** is legal rather than medical terminology and refers to psychiatric harm caused by some sudden overwhelming event so as to put the victim in fear for their life. Where harm of this nature is caused negligently, it must amount to a recognised psychiatric condition such as post-traumatic stress disorder (*Simpson v ICI*). Intentionally caused harm of this nature is regarded differently and damages will generally be available. The *locus classicus* is *Wilkinson v Downton* in which a man told a woman that her husband was "lying at The Elms with both legs broken". This was a joke, but not a very funny one as the woman became psychiatrically ill. Professor Joe Thomson analysed this case as one of fraud.

Where harm is caused negligently a critical distinction is drawn between primary and secondary victims. A primary victim is placed in personal danger. Secondary victims are those who suffer through apprehension for the safety of another. Primary victims have been able to recover damages for nervous shock since the decision in *Dulieu v R White and Sons* in 1901, although there are some earlier Scottish authorities. In *Dulieu* the Court of King's Bench allowed recovery of damages to a woman who had suffered a severe shock when a horse van was negligently driven into the bar in which she worked. The plaintiff was pregnant at the time and later gave premature birth to a child who, as the law report puts it, was "born an idiot". Following the House of Lords case of *Page v Smith*, psychiatric harm to primary victims is treated effectively as just another reparable form of personal injury. Where psychiatric harm is caused in breach of a duty of care to guard against personal injury to the pursuer, then liability will arise. *Page* involved a minor parking shunt that reactivated a pre-existing condition, myalgic encephalomyelitis (ME) in the claimant who was sitting in the car that was shunted. His health was directly affected by an act in breach of a duty of care, personal injury was within the scope of the duty and so the defendant was held liable.

While there is earlier case law on the point (see e.g. *Bourhill v Young*; *Hambrook v Stokes*), recognition that secondary victims could recover for nervous shock came in 1983 in the House of Lords case *McLoughlin v O'Brian*. In that case a woman suffered shock seeing her husband and children in a horrific condition in hospital shortly after they had been in a car accident and before they were cleaned up. One child died. Damages were awarded, but the court placed limitations on the possibility of recovery. The current rules on recovery by secondary victims are those laid down in *Alcock v Chief Constable of South Yorkshire*, the Hillsborough disaster case. No duty will arise unless: a tie of love and affection is established between the secondary and primary victim; the secondary victim is present at the event or its immediate aftermath; and perception of the event or its immediate aftermath must be direct. Direct perception means that the secondary victim must personally see or hear the event. The relatives of the victims of the disaster were unable to satisfy these conditions. Ties of love and affection may be presumed readily between spouses or parent and child, but in other relationships such ties will have to be established in evidence. Robert Alcock lost his brother-in-law, Brian Harrison lost two brothers. In the absence of evidence to show that their relationships were particularly close, neither recovered damages. Of those appellants whose ties with primary victims could be presumed, their cases failed because they could not satisfy the other requirements. Some did not arrive at the scene until some eight hours after the event and this was too late to count as presence at the aftermath. Some learned of the tragedy on television or heard about it on the radio meaning that the requirement of direct perception was not satisfied.

Subsequent case law demonstrates the difficulty facing secondary victims. In *Robertson v Forth Road Bridge Joint Board (No.2)* the pursuer watched as his workmate and drinking buddy of 20 years fell to his death and in *McFarlane v EE Caledonia Ltd* an oil worker on a supply vessel witnessed the Piper Alpha disaster. Neither recovered damages. There was a brief period during which courts allowed recovery to pursuers directly involved with incidents although without close ties of love and affection (*Salter v UB Frozen and Chilled Foods Ltd*; *Anderson v Christian Salvesen Plc*), but a return to a strict approach was apparent in *Young v McVean*. A mother on her way to meet her son passed the scene of an accident in which, unknown to her, he had died. She was denied damages because the realisation of what had happened dawned on her gradually, it was not a sudden shock. Similarly, in an English case, *Taylorson v Shieldness Produce Ltd*, parents who suffered psychiatric illness were denied damages when their child took three days to die. Where there is scope to argue the point, a pursuer has a far better chance of obtaining damages if they can be classed as a primary victim. In *Young v Charles Church (Southern) Ltd* the claimant's workmate was electrocuted when he shorted out an overhead power cable with a scaffolding pole. The claimant was held by the Court of Appeal to have been within the area of physical danger and so recovered damages as a primary victim. In *Campbell v North Lanarkshire County Council* a series of electrical explosions occurred in a room which the pursuer had just left. He returned to assist colleagues with whom he had been working. The nature of their injuries meant they were in a ghastly state. The event was continuing on the pursuer's return and he contended that he felt himself in danger. Proof before answer was allowed to establish whether he was a primary or secondary victim. The law in this area is not regarded as satisfactory, but, while various proposals for reform have been advanced, they are yet to be implemented.

BREACH OF STATUTORY DUTY

Many duties are imposed by Act of Parliament. Some understanding of the **3–05** relation between the common law and statute is essential in this area. The question that arises is whether the neglect of statutory duties or negligence in their exercise gives rise to civil liability to a party who suffers as a consequence. The general rule is that the existence of a statutory duty does not of itself give rise to civil liability. The question must be addressed with reference to the provisions of the particular statute. There are three possibilities: the Act may provide that civil liability arises; it may exclude civil liability; or it may be silent on the point. These three alternatives invoke different considerations.

Where the Act provides for civil liability, claims may proceed on the basis of the statute. This is the case, for example, with the Occupiers' Liability (Scotland) Act 1960, the Animals (Scotland) Act 1987 and the Consumer Protection Act 1987. If claims at common law have not been specifically excluded, then such claims may also be brought as an alternative to the statutory claim, provided of course that a common law duty is in place. A statutory duty will not create a common law duty where there was none before. It is possible for a statutory claim to succeed while the common law claim fails and vice versa.

Where the Act imposes a duty, but excludes civil liability then no statutory claim may be brought for breach. Nevertheless, a common law claim may be raised, but only where an equivalent duty is recognised at common law. This occurs typically with industrial safety legislation, so, while s.47 of the Health and Safety at Work Act 1974 excludes civil liability, breaches of the duty to provide a safe working environment will be pursued at common law.

Where the Act is silent on civil liability three presumptions operate. First, where a specific mode of enforcement is specified or a criminal sanction imposed for breach, no civil liability arises in addition. The exception is where a duty is imposed for the benefit of a person or class of persons of which the pursuer is a member, the typical example being industrial safety legislation passed for the benefit of employees. Second, where no mode of enforcement is prescribed civil liability will arise. Third, statute will create no additional right of action where an existing private law remedy is available.

Presumptions are, however, only presumptions and when contested the intention of Parliament must be determined. The whole Act may be construed and pre-existing law taken into consideration. It is relevant to consider the loss contemplated by Parliament. In *Gorris v Scott* the plaintiff was unable to sue for breach of regulations intended to prevent contagion of disease when his un-penned sheep were swept overboard at sea. It is relevant to consider whether the duty was intended to benefit the pursuer. In *Cutler v Wandsworth Stadium Ltd* a bookmaker failed to obtain damages when no space was made available for him at the dog track in breach of the Betting and Lotteries Act 1934 s.11(2). The Act was passed for the orderly regulation of places of entertainment in general and not for the benefit of bookmakers in particular (see also *Pullar v Window Clean Ltd*). It is also relevant to consider the availability of other remedies. This was a significant consideration in *Murphy v Brentwood District Council* in which a local authority was not held liability to the eventual purchaser for approval of flawed plans for building foundations. The plaintiff had recovered most of his losses from insurance so liability would simply have meant shifting losses between insurance companies. The Building (Scotland) Act 2003 s.511 now provides for civil liability for failure to comply with building regulations.

LIABILITY OF PUBLIC BODIES

3–06 Statutory powers and duties provide much of the legal basis on which public bodies act. The potential liability of public bodies give rise to particular considerations because of the nature of the powers and duties conferred on them. This remains the case even though the distinction that was drawn between the exercise of discretion on broad policy matters and at operational level has now been abandoned. The Supreme Court held in *Robinson v Chief Constable of West Yorkshire* that the general principles of negligence apply to public authorities in the same way that they apply to public individuals. Decisions on civil liability for negligence in the exercise of statutory powers are particularly susceptible to policy considerations where the defender is a public body and, of course, where liability is recognised, the public purse bears the burden of loss.

Courts are, in general, reluctant to impose civil liability in circumstances that would inhibit or discourage public bodies in the discharge of their functions. Bodies exercising regulatory functions are generally not liable to those who suffer loss as a consequence. See, for example, *Yuen Kun Yeu v Attorney General of Hong Kong* where no duty was owed by Commissioner of Deposit Taking Companies to individual depositors, and *Harris v Evans*, where no duty was owed by the local authority acting on the advice of health and safety inspector to the operators of a crane used for bungee jumping who had lost business. When taking children into care for their own safety *D v East Berkshire Community Health Trust* established that a duty of care is owed the child, but not the parents thus avoiding the conflict of interest that would occur were the interests of parents taken into account in circumstances where the welfare of the child is paramount. Similarly, in *Jain v Trent Strategic Health Authority* no duty of care was owed the operators of a nursing home whose registration was withdrawn in the interests of the elderly residents even though, in the event, the concerns raised against the home had proved unfounded.

The fact that powers are conferred on a body for the safety of the public does not in itself indicate a duty of care to prevent injury. In *Stovin v Wise* the local authority had statutory powers to remove dangers from roads. By a majority decision of the House of Lords no duty was owed a motorcyclist who was seriously injured when a car pulled out across his path. The driver's view had been obscured by a bank which was known to the authority to make the junction dangerous. Similarly, in *Gorringe v Calderdale* there was no common law duty to paint warning signs on a road although the authority had the power to do so. Lord Rodger remarked in that case that, "the common law of Scotland is somewhat more generous to those injured due to the failure to maintain the roads than was the English common law". The Scottish position was reviewed and affirmed in the Inner House in *Macdonald v Aberdeenshire County Council*. In Scotland a common law duty may be imposed on a roads authority in respect of a known hazard which creates a foreseeable risk of an accident. This was not established in *Macdonald*, which was factually similar to *Gorringe*. A road accident was attributed by the pursuer to worn road markings and an obscure give way sign at a junction, but Lady Paton held that, in the absence of previous complaints, accidents or near misses, the state of the road was not a hazard of which the defenders were aware and an accident was not reasonably foreseeable. By contrast, in *Bowes v Highland Regional Council* the road authority was liable when the parapet of a bridge gave way and a driver drowned as his pick-up truck fell into the Kyle of Tongue below. The dangerous state of the parapet had been made known to the authority some five years previously and a scheme to monitor its condition implemented, but discontinued. The difficulty in the case is the question of whether the accident was caused by the parapet since the accident would not have happened had the driver not lost control of his vehicle in the first place. In *Dewar v Scottish Borders Council* the pursuer attributed a motorcycle accident to the dangerous state of the carriageway. The defender is this instance had a fairly rigorous system for inspecting and maintaining roads and negligence was not established. While the Scots position differs from the English, the extent of the difference is limited to known hazards and foreseeable accidents. In *Ryder v Highland Council* the authority was not liable for a road accident attributed to a failure to grit the road.

The jurisdictional difference noted above is strengthened by recent judicial affirmation. If there is a broad tendency, it has been towards the eradication of such differences in negligence with the process not confined to courts located in England. In *A&J Allan (Blairnyle) Ltd v Strathclyde Fire Board* the extent of the duty owed by a fire service to a property owner was considered in the Inner House. Having extinguished a fire at a farm the fire brigade left only for another fire to break out later from smouldering embers in an adjacent building. Scottish authorities that would have supported liability in these circumstances, *Burnett v Grampian Fire and Rescue Service*, *Duff v Highland and Islands Fire Board* and *Gibson v Chief Constable of Strathclyde*, were disapproved. The English case, *Capital and Counties Plc v Hampshire County Council* was followed. On this authority the duty of a fire brigade attending an emergency extends only to not making matters worse. Recalling the decision in *Michael v Chief Constable of South Wales*, the civil liability of the ambulance service appears out of step in comparison to other emergency services. In *Kent v Griffiths* it was held that an ambulance crew owed a duty to arrive on the scene of an accident within a reasonable time. Having accepted the call, they had assumed responsibility and were liable in damages when the plaintiff suffered brain damage as a result of their delay. Proof before answer was allowed in *Aitken v Scottish Ambulance Service* in which a child died after the ambulance attending was 21 minutes late.

NOVEL CIRCUMSTANCES

3–07 Novel circumstances arise where there is no clear precedent for a duty of care because either the relationship between the parties is not one that has been recognised as giving rise to a duty or the harm is not of a type that has been recognised or excluded as the subject of a duty of care. Novel cases seem to arise most often where the defenders are public bodies, although of course they are by no means confined in this way. Between 1995 and 2018 the courts applied the rule in *Caparo v Dickman* as a tri-partite test to recognise or deny a duty of care in a wide variety of circumstances. There had to be foreseeability of harm, a relationship of proximity between the parties and it had to be fair, just and reasonable to impose a duty on the defender. While these factors continue to be relevant, a change of approach was signalled in the Supreme Court case of *Robinson v Chief Constable of West Yorkshire*. In *Robinson* police officers who arrested a suspect in the street where pedestrians were passing were liable to a frail elderly lady who found herself at the bottom of a ruck involving two sturdy officers and a struggling suspected drug dealer. Lord Reed revisited Lord Bridge's speech in *Caparo* and held that the tri-partite test was misconstrued. Foreseeability and proximity are central to liability in negligence and considerations of justice and policy always inform deliberations on the existence of a duty. These factors are taken together in questions of negligence, they are no longer to be regarded as separable components of a test. As Lord Reed explained:

> "In the ordinary run of cases, courts consider what has been decided previously and follow the precedents (unless it is necessary to consider whether the precedents should be departed from). In cases where the question of whether a duty of care arises has not previously been decided, the courts will consider the closest analogies in the existing law, with a view to maintaining the coherence of the law and the avoidance of inappropriate distinctions. They will also weigh up the reasons for and against imposing liability, in order to decide whether the existence of a duty of care would be just and reasonable."

Applying the general principles of negligence, the recognition of duties of care in novel circumstances depends on extending or departing from existing precedents that most closely fit the circumstances or on the basis of an assumption of responsibility as determined by the court. It is only in novel circumstances that policy considerations should form a distinct element of the court's reasoning.

4. PERSONALITY RIGHTS

DEFAMATION

4–01 There are few areas of delict that readily provide such scope for discussion. Defamation is a delict that is invoked to protect reputation. It is a wrong normally constituted by harmful words, spoken or written, although defamatory inferences may be drawn from conduct (see e.g. *Monson v Tussauds*). Interdict or interim interdict may be sought to prevent dissemination of defamatory statements. Claims for damages arise where such a statement has been made, every repetition of a defamatory statement is a new wrong and actionable. It is not, in Scotland and at present, necessary to demonstrate actual losses; affront is sufficient harm. This explains the lack of any requirement for the statement to have been communicated to a third party. Communication of the statement is necessary, but the requirement for communication can be satisfied by communication to the pursuer alone (*Ramsay v Maclay*). The sufficiency of affront for an award of damages may be largely attributable to the role played in the development of the law by the old Roman action for insult, the *actio injuriarum*.

Professor Kenneth Norrie has identified a period between the late 19th and early 20th centuries as the time in which Scots resorted most frequently to defamation litigation. There are social historical reasons for this, but it may be said that this was the period during which Scots clearly felt that a slur on reputation was something worth litigating over. In more modern times such litigation has become largely, though not entirely, the preserve of the rich and famous. Partly this is an access to justice issue—defamation litigation is an expensive business, even though Scotland has never seen the inflated levels of damages awarded in England, (or the inflated fees charged by some of the celebrated English libel firms … note, specialist firms now refer to this area of practice as "reputation management"), but also because social standing appears no longer to be the issue that it was even 50 years ago. Society may no longer be stratified in the ways that it has been in the past and people may no longer be so acutely conscious of their place in the general scheme of things and therefore sensitive to slurs on character. Nevertheless, statements can still be genuinely and seriously damaging. Imagine, for example, that all your neighbours have been led to believe, wrongly, that you are an active paedophile.

The internet of course has presented the law with new challenges, not least with the rapidity and breadth of dissemination now possible. Where reputations exist largely online, in some cases with considerable financial value attached to them, the extent to which the old protections can adapt to new circumstances is a moot point. *Lord McAlpine of West Green v Bercow* may serve as a warning to those issuing "witty" tweets where serious and damaging allegations are concerned, but internet phenomena such as trolling raise more issues than are likely to be met entirely by re-modelling old law on defamation, though adaptation and reform of the present law is at least a start.

Some re-modelling of the law has indeed taken place and this may perhaps best be regarded as a work in progress. England and Wales codified their law in the Defamation Act 2013. Very little of this Act applies in Scotland, but the Scottish Law Commission has recently concluded a report on defamation (Scot Law Com Report No.248, 2017) to which is appended a draft Bill. Whether this Bill will be introduced in the Scottish Parliament in something like its present form or indeed at all is not known, but it seems highly likely that there will be some substantial changes made during the shelf-life of the present text.

One further point needs making before the substantive law is considered. While defamation provides means of redress for wrongful damage to reputation, this is only one side of the coin. Litigation or the threat of litigation is often used to stifle criticism, that is to silence those whose statements are unwelcome. In principle, when a statement can be justified the person making it should perhaps stick to their guns. There is after all a range of possible defences available. Electing to defend an action is, however, a calculated gamble and the financial consequences of an unsuccessful defence, or even of entering into litigation at all, may suffice in many cases to silence the speaker. The law is faced with a difficult job in balancing freedom of speech on one hand with the right to reputation on the other.

Establishing defamation
Defamation has been described as: 4–02

"[T]he wrong or delict which is committed when a person makes an injurious and false imputation, conveyed by words or signs, against the character or reputation of another. Character or reputation must be here understood in the widest sense to include moral and social reputation and financial credit" (F.T. Cooper, *The Law of Defamation and Verbal Injury*, 2nd edn, 1906).

For a successful action, two points must be established by the pursuer. First, the statement complained of must be capable of bearing a defamatory meaning, in short it must have defamatory capacity. This is a question of law to be determined by the court. Second, the pursuer must have been defamed. This is a question of fact to be determined at proof or by a jury.

Where the defamatory capacity of a statement is established, it is assumed to be false and to have been made *animus iniuriandi*, that is with the intention of causing harm. There is no requirement on the pursuer to establish *culpa*, because malice and falsity are inferred from defamatory capacity. Liability then is effectively strict. Consequently, liability may be incurred without there ever having been any intent to harm. The classic example of innocent defamation is the case of *Hulton v Jones*, in which the author of a novel created a fictional character with the unlikely name of Artemus Jones. This Artemus Jones was a churchwarden from Peckham who absconded to France with a lady who was not his wife. Unfortunately for the author, there was a real Artemus Jones. Doubly unfortunate was the fact that Artemus Jones was a barrister. The defendant was liable in £1,750 damages, a substantial sum at the time, since the plaintiff convinced the court that readers would understand the story as referring to him. The innocence of this defamation may be open to question since the real Artemus Jones had been employed previously as a sub-editor at the *Sunday Chronicle*, the newspaper which published the story.

It is not, moreover, for the pursuer to establish that the statement complained of is false. If the statement is true then it cannot be defamatory since defamatory statements are, by definition, false, but the truth of an allegation is for the defender to prove by running the defence of *veritas*. A statement may have defamatory capacity where the imputation is one of immorality, criminality, dishonesty, financial unsoundness, fitness for office or where negative aspersions are cast on the pursuer's professional, vocational or business competence. There is no definitive list, but these are typical examples. It should be noted that corporate bodies may raise actions as indeed may unincorporated associations, but not local authorities (*Derbyshire CC v Times Newspapers Ltd*).

A test for defamatory capacity is provided by a dictum of Lord Atkin in *Sim v Stretch*: "Would the words tend to lower the plaintiff in the estimation of right-thinking members of society generally?" This serves as a guideline, and its advantage is that it is flexible and allows for notions of what is defamatory to change over time, but it does not work terribly well where the allegation is of financial unsoundness. The test is objective. The issue is not what the pursuer understands the words to mean, neither is it relevant to consider what the defender meant by the words. Whether a statement is defamatory is determined by the views of "right-thinking" people. Of course, the court determines what "right-thinking" people think. "Right-thinking" people are reasonable persons who do not hold prejudices.

A statement may be clearly defamatory or it may contain a defamatory innuendo. For example, the statement that X is a thief is prima facie defamatory. The statement that X holds a surprising quantity of electronic goods in a lock up garage is not. X, however, may find the latter statement objectionable on the basis that it contains the suggestion that X is either a thief or deals in stolen goods. If X pursues the matter the onus lies on them to establish that the statement complained of bears such an innuendo.

If the defamatory capacity of the statement is established the pursuer must then establish that they have in fact been defamed by it. The statement must have been understood as referring to the pursuer and, where innuendo is pled, it must have been understood as bearing the meaning contended for by the pursuer. As Lord Anderson put it in *Duncan v Associated Scottish Newspapers Ltd*, the question that must be asked is:

"[W]ould a reasonable man, reading the publication complained of, discover in it matter defamatory of the pursuer? Or, put otherwise, the question is, what meaning would the ordinary reader of the newspaper put upon the paragraph which the pursuer complained of?"

While this appears to suggest an objective approach, the context and circumstances of publication are taken into account. What must be determined is how the words are likely to be understood by those people likely to have heard or read them. Simple abuse is not defamatory since abuse will generally be understood as such. Equally satire is not actionable as defamation. Words spoken *in rixa*, that is in anger, in the heat of the moment are also likely to be understood as not seriously intended and therefore not defamatory. In *Christie v Robertson* a misunderstanding arose at an auction when two men both thought they had bought the same horse. When one of them led it away a quarrel ensued in which one man said of the other that he "should have been in the hands of the police 20 times in the last five years". The action failed, but the result might have gone the other way had the comments been made in writing. In the colourful case of *Harper v Fernie* the female pursuer got no damages when called a "damned drunken old whore" during a heated altercation with a neighbour.

Defences
Faced with an action for defamation the defender may dispute the substance 4–03 of the claim, denying that they spoke the words or issued the statement or maintaining that the statement did not refer to the pursuer and could not reasonably be understood as referring to them. Equally it may be argued that the words were not capable of bearing the defamatory meaning attributed to them by the pursuer. Where such arguments fail, the defender has a number of specific defences available. The election to use any given defence will depend on the circumstances.

Veritas convicii excusat
Since by definition a defamatory statement is untrue, *veritas* (truth) affords 4–04 a complete defence at common law. The onus is on the defender to prove the truth of the allegation. Under the Defamation Act 1952 s.5, the defender need only prove the truth of those facts which are defamatory; other facts, which do not materially affect the reputation of the pursuer need not be proved. When applied successfully this defence rebuts the presumption of falsity. Where the defence does not succeed, this may justify an award of substantial damages, as seen in *Baigent v BBC*. Serious allegations concerning the running of a nursing home had been broadcast. The defenders offered to prove the truth of the allegations, but failed to do so. A contrary example may be found in *Gecas v Scottish Television*. The action was brought by a party accused of involvement in the liquidation of Jews during the Second World War. This case was successfully defended since the allegations could be shown to be true.

Fair comment

4–05 A great deal of latitude is given people to express opinions or comment on matters in the public interest. Of course, the expression of an opinion or comment is not the same thing as a statement of fact. Nevertheless, opinions and comments may be found objectionable if they are perceived as damaging to the subject's reputation. Comments on all sorts of matters are made all the time on TV, in newspapers, on blogs and social media. Perhaps the classic example is comments made when reviewing locations, products, art, services or events. Fair comment is a common law defence applying where certain criteria are met. First, the subject of the comment must be a matter in the public interest. The threshold for public interest is not set high and probably excludes only private and personal matters as this dictum of Lord Denning in *London Artists v Littler* suggests:

> "Whenever a matter is such as to affect people at large, so that they may be legitimately interested in, or concerned at, what is going on; or what may happen to them or to others; then it is a matter of public interest on which everybody is entitled to make fair comment."

Second, the comment must be based on facts. "The comment must explicitly or implicitly indicate, at least in general terms, the facts upon which it is based" per Lord Phillips in the Supreme Court case *Spiller v Joseph*. Third, the facts must be truly stated. The onus is on the defender to establish this. The Defamation Act 1952 s.6 provides that the defence will be good if the facts upon which the opinion is based are true even if there are other facts which are not true, so long as these unproved facts do not themselves amount to a defamatory allegation.

Provided these criteria are met then the defence will succeed. The idea is that the reading, listening or viewing public may make their own judgement on the validity of any comment or opinion when presented with the facts upon which the comment is made. Comments do not really have to be entirely fair, they can be overstated, eccentric or simply rude. As Lord McLaren stated in *Archer v Ritchie & Co*:

> "The expression of an opinion as to a state of facts truly set forth is not actionable, even when that opinion is couched in vituperative or contumelious language."

Absolute privilege

4–06 The defence of absolute privilege attaches to certain circumstances or occasions as a matter of law where the public interest in freedom of speech over-rides any personal interest in reputation. Absolute privilege is a common law defence, but it applies in some circumstances by virtue of statutory provisions. Where statements are absolutely privileged any action for defamation will be irrelevant. Absolute privilege applies to statements made in the Westminster Parliament, whether these are made by MPs or by others, such as witnesses before Select Committees. Absolute privilege also applies to reports and other papers issued under the authority of Parliament, including the reports of parliamentary proceedings in *Hansard*. The defence applies equally to proceedings before the Scottish Parliament and reports and papers authorised by it under the Scotland Act 1998 s.41. Ministers of the Crown are afforded absolute privilege in the proper exercise of their functions. The Defamation Act 1996 s.13 provides for waiver of privilege by an MP or other person who may see some benefit in the matter coming before the courts

Judicial proceedings also attract absolute privilege, although here the protection afforded is less than in the case of parliamentary proceedings as privilege may be lost where statements are made that are not relevant to the proceedings. The common law attaches absolute privilege to the written and oral statements of judges, pleaders and witnesses, but not to the parties themselves whose statements are afforded the lesser protection of qualified privilege. The protection granted to judicial proceedings extends also to quasi-judicial proceedings and tribunals, such as public enquiries, employment appeal tribunals and children's hearings. The Defamation Act 1996 s.14 provides that fair and accurate reports of court proceedings published contemporaneously are absolutely privileged. Again, children's hearings, employment appeal tribunals and public enquiries are included along with all UK courts, the European Court of Justice, the European Court of Human Rights and International Criminal Tribunals.

Qualified privilege
Similar to absolute privilege, qualified privilege is a common law defence **4–07** that is imposed on certain occasions by statute. The common law defence does not, however, depend on a fixed range of circumstances, but arises more generally, whenever a statement is made in response to a duty. The recipient of the communication must have an interest in hearing it. As Lord Atkinson stated in *Adam v Ward*:

"A privileged occasion is ... an occasion where the person who makes a communication has an interest or a duty, legal, social or moral, to make it to the person to whom it is made, and the person to whom it is so made has a corresponding interest or duty to receive it. This reciprocity is essential."

When qualified privilege applies the presumption of malice is displaced. This is because malice is no longer the natural inference to be drawn from the making of the statement. The effect of this is that the pursuer must prove *animus injuriandi*, that is intent to injure. This may place a considerable burden on the pursuer and so this defence considerably strengthens the position of the defender, but it is not a complete defence. The defence will fail if the pursuer can show either that the statement was made with intent to injure, that is maliciously, or if the defender had no honest belief in the truth of the statement. In *Horrocks v Lowe* Lord Diplock explained, "[i]f it be proved that he did not believe that what he published was true this is generally conclusive evidence of express malice". The working of the defence may be seen in the House of Lords case *Fraser v Mirza*. The pursuer was charged with an offence by a police officer. The pursuer wrote a letter of complaint to the chief constable in which he accused the officer of racial motives. The officer sued and the pursuer ran the defence of qualified privilege. The defence applied since making a complaint through the proper channels satisfies both the requirement that the statement is made in pursuit of a duty to do so and is directed at a person with a legitimate interest in hearing the complaint. The defence, however, failed because it was established in evidence that the pursuer had no basis for his expressed view that the officer was racially motivated.

Consider the following example. X makes an allegation to the police that Y is abusing his children. Y sues in defamation. X pleads qualified privilege. There is little doubt that X is under a social and moral duty to bring such a concern to the relevant authorities even though, strictly speaking, X is under no legal obligation to report crime. The court agrees there is a duty, accordingly X's communication is privileged. If X's allegation is honestly made, the defence succeeds, even though criminal investigation does not find evidence or sufficient evidence to conclude that the children have indeed been abused. If X's allegation is malicious then X will be liable in damages, but only if Y can prove intent to injure. One way Y could do this is to establish that his children live in South America, he has no contact with them and these facts are known to X. It follows that X could not have believed in the truth of the allegations and so intent to injure may be inferred. Had X made the allegation not to the police, but to other neighbours, qualified privilege would not apply. Unlike the police, the neighbours have no legitimate interest in receiving the information.

The press and media in general have a duty to the public to inform. Certain types of reporting are accorded qualified privilege by the Defamation Act 1996 s.15 and Sch.1. The schedule contains a long list covering reports of the deliberations of various types of body, including council committee meetings, associations for promoting sports, arts, sciences and so on. The defence is lost if the pursuer can show that the defender: a) was requested by the pursuer to publish in a suitable manner a reasonable letter or statement by way of explanation or contradiction; and b) the defender refused to do so (s.15(2)).

One important provision in the Defamation Act 2013 that does apply in Scotland is s.6. This accords qualified privilege on a peer reviewed statement in a scientific or academic journal. This is significant because it is not unknown for corporate interests to resort to defamation litigation in the process of repressing research findings that may damage sales or bring their product into disrepute.

Fair retort

4–08 If an allegation is made against a person that person is entitled to reply. If the reply contains defamatory elements then it may found an action for defamation, but there is no presumption of malice because the motivation behind the statement is to protect the defender's own reputation. Therefore, where fair retort applies, the pursuer will have to prove intent to injure on the part of the defender. Fair retort then may be seen as a species of qualified privilege. Successful use of this defence may be seen, for example, in *Gray v SSPCA*, in which the defenders responded to an accusation of cruel injustice published in a local newspaper by repeating the substance of complaints they had brought against the purser, a farmer and in respect of which he had been prosecuted, but found not proven. The defenders also pointed out to the readership the difference between a not proven and not guilty verdict. In order to count as a fair retort, the reply must be kept within the bounds of relevance. In *Blair v Eastwood* the defender overstepped the boundaries of fair retort when he was accused by the pursuer of having fathered her child. He in turn accused the pursuer of having had sex with at least two other men. This was not a fair retort.

The *Reynolds* defence of responsible journalism

Aside from circumstances in which privilege operates, the media is given **4–09** considerable protection by the defence of fair comment. Fair comment, however, depends on facts being accurately stated. *Veritas* depends on facts being true. The *Reynolds* defence operates, in the public interest in being informed and in the interests of freedom of speech, to provide protection in circumstances where the publisher is uncertain of all the facts. In *Reynolds v The Times Newspapers* certain defamatory allegations were published concerning the plaintiff who had just resigned as Taoiseach of the Republic of Ireland. The reasons for the resignation were clearly a matter of public interest and the defendants sought the extension of privilege to political information in general.

The House of Lords did not grant the defendants the defence asked for, but formulated something that was at first viewed as a development on privilege, but which developed into a new defence. The effect of the defence is that unproven allegations may be published where there is a duty to do so and a corresponding right on the part of the public to know. Where the defence applies, it is not open to the pursuer to offer to prove intent to injure. This was established by the House of Lords in *Jameel v Wall Street Journal*. The conditions that have to be met for the defence to apply are such as to establish the propriety of the defender's behaviour and exclude malice.

A 10 point guide to the factors to be considered was set down by Lord Nicholls in *Reynolds*. Although there was an attempt, in *Loutchansky v Times Newspapers*, to have these factors treated as strict tests, the Court of Appeal in that case made it clear that they were not to be applied in that way, but were factors indicating the ingredients of "responsible journalism". Lord Nicholls' guide follows:

"Depending on the circumstances, the matters to be taken into account include the following. The comments are illustrative only. 1. The seriousness of the allegation. The more serious the charge, the more the public is misinformed and the individual harmed, if the allegation is not true. 2. The nature of the information, and the extent to which the subject matter is a matter of public concern. 3. The source of the information. Some informants have no direct knowledge of the events. Some have their own axes to grind, or are being paid for their stories. 4. The steps taken to verify the information. 5. The status of the information. The allegation may have already been the subject of an investigation which commands respect. 6. The urgency of the matter. News is often a perishable commodity. 7. Whether comment was sought from the plaintiff. He may have information others do not possess or have not disclosed. An approach to the plaintiff will not always be necessary. 8. Whether the article contained the gist of the plaintiff's side of the story. 9. The tone of the article. A newspaper can raise queries or call for an investigation. It need not adopt allegations as statements of fact. 10. The circumstances of the publication, including the timing."

These factors were resolved into a three-part test by Lord Hoffmann in *Jameel*, an approach subsequently applied in the Supreme Court in *Flood v Times Newspapers*. Is the subject matter of public interest? Is the inclusion of the defamatory statement justifiable? Were the steps taken to gather and publish the information fair and reasonable? The current status of the defence in Scots law is slightly curious. It is a creation of English jurisprudence and was recognised in Scotland in *Adams v Guardian Newspapers Ltd*, albeit the defence was not upheld in that case. It has since been abolished in England and Wales and replaced in s.4 of the Defamation Act 2013 by a defence of publication in the public interest. A similar development in Scotland may be anticipated, but at the time of writing the law is probably best represented by the English case law prior to the 2013 Act.

Defamation Act 1996

4–10 Because liability attaches to every repeat of a defamatory statement some protection is needed for those who are involved in dissemination, but who have no responsibility for content such as newspaper vendors or distributors. Section 1(1) of the Defamation Act 1996 provides that a person has a defence if they show that: (a) they were not the author, editor or publisher of the statement; (b) they took reasonable care in relation to its publication; and (c) they did not know, and had no reason to know, that what they did caused or contributed to the publication of a defamatory statement. Section 1(2) and (3) provide interpretation on the meanings of author, editor or publisher, notably the originator of a statement is not the author if they did not intend it to be published. Those with no responsibility for publication, such as persons involved in the production process, are protected by this defence. Those who do have responsibility for publication are only protected to the extent that they have taken reasonable care. Reasonable care is elaborated in s.1(5). Where the defender is the author, editor or publisher, then the s.1 defence is not available and the choice will have to be made whether to defend the position or make an offer of amends as provided for under s.2.

Clearly the s.1 defence may be relied upon by internet intermediaries, that is parties hosting material published by others on the internet. The protection afforded by the defence may, however, be lost once the intermediary is put on notice of the defamatory nature of the material hosted. In this case the material ought to be removed as soon as practicable. In *Godfrey v Demon Internet* a defamatory posting was held on the defendant's news server from which it was available for download. It was held that the defendant was not a commercial publisher, but having failed to remove the offending material they could not be said to have exercised reasonable care and so the s.1 defence failed. In a similar case before the Court of Appeal, *Payim Tamiz v Google*, the offending material was removed within three days of the defendant being put on notice. This was deemed to show reasonable care and any harm done in the short period before removal would have been trivial. The defence succeeded.

Internet service providers are given some protection against civil liability and criminal charges by the Electronic Commerce (EC Directive) Regulations 2002. There are three different levels of protection dependent on the control exercisable over material. Under reg.17, providers who operate as a conduit for information only are immune from civil liability. Under reg.18, providers who cache information are protected provided certain conditions are met. They must not modify information, they must comply with industry standards on access to and updating information and they must respond expeditiously to removal or disablement of access to information at source. Under reg.19, providers who host information are protected where they have no actual knowledge of unlawful activity or information and no awareness of facts or circumstances that would have made this apparent. On discovering the defamatory nature of material, they must respond expeditiously to remove it or disable access to it.

Offer to make amends

The 1996 Act s.2 makes provision for an offer of amends. This offer can be **4–11** made to the pursuer whether the defamation has occurred innocently or not, but it does imply an admission of liability. An offer is made to correct the statement, publish an apology and pay compensation. Like any offer, it can be accepted or rejected. Acceptance ends proceedings, but s.3 makes provision for enforcement and for determination of terms not agreed upon. If the offer is rejected then the fact that one was made may be used as a defence under s.4. This defence precludes the use of other defences. This is a good defence provided the defender had no grounds for believing that the statement was defamatory of the pursuer. This, indeed, will be presumed to be the case, the onus falls on the pursuer to rebut the presumption by proving intent to injure, see s.4(3) and *Milne v Express Newspapers*.

VERBAL INJURY

4–12 Verbal injury provides a ground of action separate from defamation. The critical differences between defamation and verbal injury may be simply stated. Verbal injury is the appropriate form of action where a reputation has been harmed by words, spoken or written, that are not defamatory. The form of *culpa* that is relevant for liability is malice, but, unlike defamation, malice is not presumed. As the statement is not defamatory there is no basis for any such presumption. Therefore, malice must be averred and proved. Furthermore, a verbal injury is not actionable unless the statement complained of is false. Again, because the statement is not defamatory there is no basis for a presumption of falsity. Accordingly, the onus lies on the pursuer to prove that the statement complained of is false. Losses must be clearly established. A case in verbal injury is therefore difficult to establish and modern cases are relatively rare. A brief outline here will suffice.

It is convenient to present verbal injury as falling into three categories: verbal injury affecting business; false statements with the intention of exposing the pursuer to hatred, contempt and ridicule; and, finally, slander on a third party. The continuing relevance of the last category may be in doubt. It is based on a case from 1857, *North of Scotland Banking Co v Duncan*, and there has never been a case in which damages have been awarded. Verbal injury affecting business involves slander of title, slander of property or falsehood causing business loss. Slander of title arises where doubt has been cast on the right of the pursuer to sell goods. On top of proving malice, the pursuer may face a difficult task in proving lost sales opportunities. Slander of property involves disparagement of the pursuer's property or goods. The best-known example is *Bruce v JM Smith* in which a property developer sued after publication of material questioning the security of his foundations. The leading case on falsehood causing business loss is *Steele v Scottish Daily Record* in which a car dealer was accused of sharp practices.

Where it can be shown that a false statement was intended to hold the subject up to hatred, contempt and ridicule, damages in the form of *solatium* are available and, of course, any patrimonial losses may be recovered. There must be some element of public hatred; ridicule on its own will not found an action. This form of verbal injury developed out of cases brought during the mid-19th century by (locally) public figures, such as teachers, ministers and politicians. In *Paterson v Welch* unpopular views were ascribed to the pursuer—class prejudice or snobbery—resulting in an upsurge of local feeling against him. He was burnt in effigy outside his home. He lost his seat at the following election and sued in verbal injury.

PRIVACY

Breach of confidence
While defamation protects or provides redress against the dissemination of **4–13**
harmful untruths It is a delict to publish or otherwise disseminate confidential
information. The *locus classicus* is *Prince Albert v Strange*. Copperplates
made by Prince Albert and Queen Victoria were entrusted to a printer. An
employee made unauthorised copies and these were sold to the defendant
who intended to display them and publish a catalogue with descriptions.
Prince Albert succeeded in gaining an injunction against further publication
and a court order requiring remaining copies to be destroyed. While personal
information is covered, much of the case law is concerned with information
attained in the course of employment, trade secrets for example. The
dissemination of such information may be prevented through use of
contractual terms known as restrictive covenants. Such terms survive the
termination of the contract of employment and are enforceable to the extent
that they are reasonably necessary to protect the business interests of the
employer.

In the absence of contractual duty recourse may be had to delict. The
traditional formulation of the law was that information divulged in confidence
or gained from a relationship of confidence, such as between banker and
client, solicitor and client or doctor and patient, could be protected. The
modern requirements for breach of confidence were set down in *Coco v AN
Clark (Engineers) Ltd*. First, the information must have the necessary quality
of confidence about it, that is it must not be in the public domain. The fact that
the information is not entirely secret does not prevent it from being
confidential. Second, the defender must be under a duty of confidence. Such
a duty may arise out of a relationship of trust but may also be recognised
where improper means have been used to attain the information, where
phones have been bugged for instance, or indeed where it is clear that the
information is confidential (see Lord Goff in *AG v Guardian Newspapers
(No 2)* [1990] 1 A.C. 109 at [282]). The third requirement is that the defender
must have made unauthorised use of the information.

The case of *Douglas v Hello!* shows the imposition of a duty of
confidentiality by contractual means. Michael Douglas and Catherine Zeta-
Jones granted exclusive rights to publish their wedding photographs to *OK!*
magazine. Under the terms of the contract the Douglases were to take all
reasonable steps to restrict access to their wedding to prevent other media
from obtaining pictures and guests were asked not to do so. A freelance
photographer infiltrated proceedings and took photographs that *Hello!*
magazine then published. In the House of Lords, it was held by a majority that
the pictures were confidential and of commercial value and that there was no
policy reason why *OK!* should not be able to protect the rights they had
acquired under contract against *Hello!* Damages of over £1 million were
awarded to *OK!* The happy couple was awarded £15,000 in respect of
interference with the residual right they had retained to veto the use of any
particular pictures by *OK!*

Misuse of private information

4–14 Article 8 of the European Convention on Human Rights states:

> "1. Everyone has the right to respect for his private and family life, his home and his correspondence. 2. There shall be no interference by a public authority with the exercise of this right except such as in accordance with the law and is necessary in a democratic society in the interests of national security, public safety or the economic well-being of the country, for the prevention of disorder or crime, for the protection of health or morals, or for the protection of the rights and freedoms of others."

The right to privacy is not an absolute right and may be over-ridden for the reasons given in art.8(2). Invasions of privacy are actionable irrespective of whether carried out by a public authority or any other body. The courts are public authorities (see Human Rights Act 1998 s.6(2) on the meaning of public authority) and they are obliged to give effect to Convention rights. In interpreting these rights courts are obliged to take into consideration inter alia relevant case law of the European Court of Human Rights, although these decisions are not binding on domestic courts (see HRA 1998 s.2). The approach taken in the UK has been to develop the common law to provide redress where rights are wrongfully invaded. English law has been remarkably reluctant to recognise invasion of privacy as a tort in its own right. Instead, the law on breach of confidence has been developed to provide redress on dissemination of material in respect of which there is "a reasonable expectation of privacy". It may be said that this has resulted in two torts, one of breach of confidence and one of misuse of private information, although they are not entirely distinct. This may clearly be seen, for example, in the case of *McKennit v Ash* in which a well-known country and western singer succeeded in preventing further publication of a book written by a friend (ex-friend presumably) that disclosed information readily classifiable as both confidential—gleaned from a relationship of confidence—and in respect of which the complainant had a reasonable expectation of privacy.

There is little or no specifically Scottish jurisprudence. Matters have not changed much since Professor Elspeth Reid observed:

> "The Scots case law on confidentiality is sparse and dominated by disputes involving trade secrets. Either the Scots have few secrets or they are good at keeping them, and when their personal confidences are betrayed these are typically published by the English media so that any litigation goes to London." ("No Sex Please, We're European" (2009) 13 Edin L.R. 116 at 120).

The starting point for misuse of private information is *Campbell v MGN*. The model Naomi Campbell claimed breach of her right to privacy when the *Mirror* published details of her drug rehabilitation treatment along with a covertly taken photograph of her leaving a group therapy session. The defendant had argued that the publication was justified in the public interest since Ms Campbell had misled the public by declaring that she did not take drugs. While it was accepted in the House of Lords that it was legitimate to establish that Ms Campbell had lied to the public, the information published was held by a 3:2 majority to be confidential and an award of damages was made. This decision was aided by the relation of the treatment to the mental and physical health of the claimant, meaning that a tenuous parallel could be drawn with medical records which are in all cases confidential. The *Campbell* case may be contrasted with *Ferdinand v MGN Ltd* in which the then England football captain was shown to have been cheating on his partner while maintaining publicly that he was a reformed character. In this case the public interest in the story was held to outweigh the claimant's right to privacy.

At the heart of misuse of private information is the interaction between two opposing Convention rights. The art.8 right to privacy, modified as it may be by the rights and freedoms of others, and the art.10 right as follows:

"1. Everyone has the right to freedom of expression. This right shall include freedom to hold opinions and to receive and impart information and ideas without interference by public authority and regardless of frontiers ... 2. The exercise of these freedoms, since it carries with it duties and responsibilities, may be subject to such formalities, conditions, restrictions or penalties as are prescribed by law and are necessary in a democratic society, in the interests of national security, territorial integrity or public safety, for the prevention of disorder or crime, for the protection of health or morals, *for the protection of the rights or reputation of others*, for preventing the disclosure of information received in confidence, or for maintaining the authority and impartiality of the judiciary" (emphasis added).

Assertion of the right to freedom of expression is the normal response to a complaint of misuse of private information. Most cases are, after all, brought against the media that has a duty to report on matters in the public interest and serves a vital role as "public watchdog" in democratic societies. Neither right takes precedence over the other and so the right to privacy must be balanced against the right to freedom of expression. In *Axel Springer AG v Germany* the European Court of Human Rights set down a list of factors that should be considered in the balancing process. Although the factors and weight to be given them will vary according to the facts at issue in the individual case, these include primarily: whether the information contributes to a debate of public interest; the public status of the claimant and their prior conduct; the method of obtaining the information and its veracity; the content, form and consequences of the publication; and the severity of the sanction (the so-called "chilling effect" of inhibitions on freedom of expression). First, the court must establish whether the pursuer's art.8 right is engaged. This is determined where there is a reasonable expectation of privacy in relation to the material in question. When, and only when the art.8 right is engaged, the court will proceed to effect a just balance between the pursuer's right to privacy and the defender's right to freedom of expression. An invasion of the claimant's art.8 right requires justification if the defender's art.10 right is to prevail.

4–15 The publication of images may amount to a delict depending on the circumstances. In *Von Hanover v Germany* Princess Caroline of Hanover was found entitled to protection against the publication of covertly taken photographs showing her going about her private business. The decisive factor in her favour was the fact that these pictures contributed nothing to any debate of public interest. By contrast the same claimant failed in a later attempt to restrain publications showing her family on a skiing holiday and her father, Prince Rainier of Monaco, clearly in ill-health. As reigning sovereign at the time of Monaco there was a public interest in the Prince's state of health that the press were entitled to report. The photographs moreover supported and illustrated the story whereas in the first case, by contrast, there was no real story at all. Publication of an image in itself will not always give rise to a remedy, as seen in *John v Associated Newspapers* in which Sir Elton John failed to obtain an interim injunction against an innocuous photograph taken of himself in the street. The consequences for the claimant were not considered significant whereas an invasion of privacy is less likely to be outweighed by freedom of expression when photographs containing children are published. This may be seen in *Murray v Express Newspapers Plc* (JK Rowling's 19 month-old son) and *Weller v Associated Newspapers Ltd* (Paul Weller's family).

Normally, a reasonable expectation of privacy will attach to lawful sexual conduct between consenting adults, although, depending on the circumstances, this may be outweighed where there is a public interest, for example in the conduct of a prominent role model as demonstrated in the *Ferdinand* case. A reasonable expectation of privacy may attach even to sexual shenanigans of a somewhat dubious nature as in *Mosley v News Group Newspapers Ltd*. Max Mosely, then president of the FIM (the governing body for Formula 1 racing) was awarded damages of £60,000 in respect of publication online of video coverage of a party at which he received the ministrations of five dominatrices dressed in Nazi uniform. Moseley was refused an injunction, the horse having well and truly bolted. The view that a reasonable expectation of privacy attaches to sexual matters even though adulterous or involving more than two people was affirmed by the Supreme Court in *PJS v News Group Newspapers Ltd*.

It is primarily, but not entirely, in the context of sexual matters that non-disclosure orders (super injunctions) may be sought in England, though not in Scotland. Such orders prevent the publication of the identity of the claimant, although since 2012 the fact that proceedings have taken place are made public. The *PJS* case concerned a review of a super-injunction that the Supreme Court held should remain in force in the interests of protecting the claimant's children. Such orders are problematic for a number of reasons, but they can act against the interests of those seeking them turning what might have been an embarrassing but short-lived tabloid splash into a matter of global interest. Inevitably, somewhere beyond the jurisdiction of domestic courts identities will be made known online and either the injunction will not be renewed on review or the claimant will end up waiving anonymity. Furthermore, maintaining secrecy through law can become prohibitively expensive. Whether the super-injunction has any real future remains to be seen.

Finally, the case of *Sir Cliff Richard OBE v BBC* demonstrates well the approach taken by the courts in such cases. A journalist within the BBC had received a tip off that an allegation of underage sex abuse had been made regarding Sir Cliff. Armed with this knowledge the journalist approached the South Yorkshire police and wrongfully exerted pressure on them to inform the BBC in advance of any search of premises. Apprehending that the BBC could blow the investigative process by publicising the investigation before they were ready to act, the police supplied the BBC with this information. The police search of Sir Cliff's home when it came was accompanied by live television coverage from a helicopter, adding drama and sensationalism to the story. Sir Cliff was never charged with any offence. He sued for invasion of privacy.

The first question for the court was whether Sir Cliff had a reasonable expectation of privacy regarding the fact that he was a suspect and the fact of the search. In view of a number of factors—the legitimate and justified wish of the claimant to avoid stigma; the consequences of wider knowledge of the fact bearing in mind the inability of some members of the public to apply the presumption of innocence to their reckonings (mud sticks) and the simple fact that it was not necessary for anyone outside the investigation to know—Mann J determined that he did. "It seems to me that on the authorities, and as a matter of principle, a suspect has a reasonable expectation of privacy in relation to a police investigation, and so I rule" (at [248]). The judge added (at [251]) that this right is not inviolable and may be displaced, for example where there is a risk to the public or where publication is made for operational reasons, neither of which applied on the present facts. Having so decided, Mann J proceeded to consider the factors as set out in *Axel Springer* at some length before balancing Sir Cliff's right to privacy against the BBC's right to freedom of expression. Given the seriousness of the consequences for the claimant an equally serious justification for the invasion of privacy by the BBC would have been required to tip the balance in favour of freedom of expression. Such justification was entirely lacking and so Sir Cliff was awarded damages. An application to appeal the decision was subsequently refused.

While this is an area of the law that will continue to develop, one fairly straightforward piece of guidance can be drawn from the case law. The publication of private information may be justified where it is relevant to support a story in the public interest. Where there is no story except for the private information, that is where the information itself is the story, then publication is less likely to be justifiable and therefore more likely to amount to an actionable wrong.

WRONGFUL DETENTION

4–16 Liberty is a reparable interest under the law of Scotland. It is also a human right. Under art.5.1 of the European Convention on Human Rights, everyone has the right to liberty and security of the person. The reparable elements are both deprivation of liberty itself and affront. Wrongful detention may also be referred to as wrongful apprehension, wrongful arrest or wrongful imprisonment, but whatever term is used it is the same delict.

The classic case is *Mackenzie v Cluny Hill Hydropathic Company* in which a female guest was detained by a hotel manager in his office for some 15 minutes. The pursuer was expected to apologise to two other guests whom she was alleged to have slighted. Any interference with physical movement can amount to detention, so while the delict may be constituted by locking a person in a room or other place from which they cannot escape, applying a physical restraint without justification is also actionable. In *Henderson v Chief Constable of Fife Police* the pursuer obtained damages having been handcuffed when she was removed by police from a laboratory during an industrial dispute despite posing no threat of escape. Her bra was also removed compounding the affront to her dignity.

Wrongful detention is a delict of intention requiring a deliberate act. Persons locked in by accident or stuck in a broken lift would have no right of action, although they might have a claim in negligence. It is not wrongful to prevent passengers from leaving an aircraft in flight or a ship at sea, nor is it wrongful to prevent passengers from leaving a train at an unscheduled stop. Detention may be justified by law, for example when a person is subject to a detention order under the Mental Health (Care and Treatment) (Scotland) Act 2003. Arrest on warrant is presumed to be justified. In these circumstances a pursuer will not succeed unless they can show malice and want of probable cause. Police have powers to detain persons without warrant on reasonable suspicion of crime for purposes of investigation or to prevent a suspect from absconding. When an action is brought in these circumstances the pursuer must aver wrongful and illegal arrest. This casts on the defender the burden of justifying their suspicions. In the absence of circumstances to justify reasonable suspicion the governing authority is *Pringle v Bremner and Stirling*. Where an arrest without warrant is carried out under statutory powers the terms of the statute will determine whether malice on the part of the defender must be shown.

ASSAULT

4–17 In civil law an assault means objectionable conduct affecting the body or dignity of the victim. Clearly a physical assault is also a crime for which a compensation order may be made in terms of the Criminal Injuries Compensation Scheme. Prosecution is not a bar to a civil action and even where no conviction has been secured a civil action may be raised. This may be seen in *Mullen v Anderson (No.2)* where civil damages were awarded in respect of a knife attack after the murder conviction failed. The explanation is that prosecution requires mens rea and proof beyond reasonable doubt. Civil liability requires intention and proof on the balance of probabilities. The requirement of intention differentiates assault from negligently inflicted injury. Intention in the context of assault was described in *Reid v Mitchell*. The action was brought by a farmworker whose shoulder was injured when he was knocked from a haycart by other workers who were larking about. Lord Young stated:

"Technically he assaulted him, although he did it playfully and without any bad intention, for if a man playfully attacks another to make him engage in sport, I am of the opinion that that us an assault, and if harm results that constitutes an actionable wrong."

Physical injury is not necessary for actionability, assault protects also wrongful interferences with dignity. Damages are available in the form of *solatium* for affront and insult (Bell, *Principles*, para.2032). In *Beaton v Drysdale* the pursuer recovered damages after he had been thrown in the harbour. In *Cock v Neville* a farmer was awarded a small sum of damages in respect of threats and abuse he had received from army officers trespassing on his land. In *Tullis v Glenday* the sum of £40 in damages was awarded to the pursuer who alleged the defender had spat in his face. The sum claimed was £500. Reasonable apprehension of physical danger will also ground an action. In *Ewing v Earl of Mar* it was held to amount to assault to ride a horse at a pedestrian, causing danger and alarm, and it was also insulting and an assault to spit at a person whether or not the phlegm found its mark. The thin skull rule operates. In *MacGregor v Shepherd* the pursuer had a septic jaw which took much longer to heal after it was broken by the defender than might normally have been anticipated. The sheriff observed that the defender was not entitled to assume his victim was in perfect health.

Actions may be defended on grounds of self-defence. This is a complete defence where established, but the actions of the defender must be reasonable. When one party to a fight over a girl hit the other over the head with a bottle, the defence failed (*Marco v Merrans*). Consent is also a defence, and were it not the courts might be full of dentists, doctors and tattoo artists. Participation in a game of golf, however, does not imply consent to being hit on the head by another player's golf ball (*Lewis v Buckpool Golf Club*). Provocation is not a complete defence, but may mitigate any sum awarded in damages where established. There must, however, be a causal link between the provocation and response. Damages were reduced in *Ross v Bryce* where the assailant had been provoked by the pursuer's verbal abuse. The pursuer had also kicked the defender's dog. (See also *Ashmore v Rock Steady Security* in which a man rather foolishly subjected a bouncer to serious verbal abuse.)

HARASSMENT

4–18 Everyone is accorded the right to be free from harassment by s.8(1) of the Protection from Harassment Act 1997. Harassment is not statutorily defined, but it includes causing alarm or distress. It must be established that the defender's conduct was intended to amount to harassment, or, viewed objectively, may reasonably be interpreted in that way. Conduct includes speech. It is not hard to think of probable instances of harassment, but the possibilities may be demonstrated by *Ferguson v British Gas*. The claimant had changed her gas supplier, but continued to receive bills from her old supplier along with threats to cut off her supply, commence legal proceedings and to report her to credit rating agencies. The refusal of the court at first instance to strike out her claim was upheld in the Court of Appeal.

A course of conduct is required for actionability, that is the objectionable behaviour must have occurred on at least two occasions. Section 8A provides an exception in cases of domestic abuse where a single event will suffice. The remedies available are interdict, interim interdict, non-harassment orders and damages. Damages are available in respect of both patrimonial losses and anxiety. A non-harassment order is viewed as being more serious and the courts will not make such an award where an interdict would be sufficient. Breach of a non-harassment order is a criminal offence. Interdict and non-harassment orders are mutually exclusive. This means that both will not be granted on the same occasion in proceedings brought under the Act, but it does not mean that a non-harassment order is unavailable where an interdict is already in place from earlier proceedings. In *McCann v McGurran* the sheriff at first instance refused a non-harassment order on the basis that there was a permanent interdict already in place against the pursuer's husband. This decision was over-ruled on appeal to the Inner House, although in the circumstances the Court found no grounds to justify a non-harassment order. Defences to an action of harassment are provided in s.8(4) and are: that the conduct was authorised by law; the conduct was pursued for the purposes of preventing or detecting crime; or the conduct was reasonable in the circumstances. In *Green v Chalmers* damages and interdict were awarded against the occupants of a neighbouring farm. The pursuer had sought advice from various bodies in respect of a rat infestation. This appears to have precipitated a campaign of harassment by her neighbours that included lighting bonfires, placing poison where the pursuer's dogs would sit, spraying her hedge and shrubs with pesticide, prolonged noisy activity in the early hours, parking large farm machinery on the boundary between the properties, sealing the lid of her septic tank with silicone sealant, placing open silage bales in the vicinity of the house and leaving a bogey packed with cattle dung for approximately 18 days.

Green v Chalmers demonstrates the effectiveness of the Act in circumstances which would once have grounded either a plea for lawburrows or a claim *in aemulationem vicini*. Both these remedies remain competent at common law, but proceedings under the Act offer a more immediately practical solution. Other non-delictual regimes that may be mobilised in cases of harassment include the quasi-administrative Antisocial Behaviour Order (ASBO), which may be sought by the Local Authority or Registered Social Landlord under the Antisocial Behaviour etc Act 2004. There are also criminal offences that may be relevant depending on the circumstances, such as the offence of threatening or abusive behaviour under s.38 of the Criminal Justice and Licensing (Scotland) Act 2010 and the offence of stalking under s.39 of the same Act.

5. NEIGHBOURHOOD

5-01   The law of neighbourhood, or neighbour law, operates in the region where delict and property law coincide. Neighbourhood law is not a well-established category in Scots law in the way that it is in, say South Africa, but is a concept found in earlier writings such as those of Hume and Bell and which surfaces every so often in judicial dicta, usually in the context of nuisance. Credit for the revival of neighbour law as a category is due largely to Professor George Gretton and Andrew Steven who use it in their text, *Property, Trusts and Succession* (Bloomsbury, 2017). Historically, it has roots in the old "guid nychtburheid" (good neighbourhood) jurisdictions of local courts long since gone; burgh magistrates, dean of guild courts and courts of barony and regality are the main examples. Neighbourhood matters such as closes blocked with refuse, dung in the streets, offensive trades usually associated with the killing and processing of animals like tanning and candlemaking and simply warring neighbours fell within this jurisdiction. Obstreperous neighbours could be "ordained to keep guid nychtburheid" and might be required to make an undertaking to do so. The other root of neighbourhood law is, of course, the common law of the realm. In this context the law of neighbourhood was understood in terms of restrictions on the freedom of owners to use their property as they wished, for example the duty to provide support for other properties where it arose or the doctrine of *aemulationem vicini* that provided for redress against malicious uses made of heritable property in order to spite neighbours. Much of what was once dealt with locally as a matter of neighbourhood now falls within local government regulation, public health and environmental law and one of the primary inhibitions on the free use of property is the requirement of planning permission for development, again, a matter of administrative law. The doctrines of support and *aemulationem vicini* persist in the common law although Protection from Harassment ought perhaps to displace the latter. The link between the old guid nychtburheid jurisdictions and the modern common law may be found in nuisance. Blocked drains, overflowing middens, noxious effusions and so on were dealt with locally as "annoyances", nuisance does not start to develop in the common law (and the English nomenclature "nuisance" is not adopted) until the mid-18th century, a time that coincides with the abolition of the old heritable jurisdictions following the defeat at Culloden, a massive growth in population, the expansion of towns and the early stages of the industrial revolution.

While there is scope for argument over the content of neighbourhood law, a traditional approach is followed in the present text and the coverage is concerned with interferences with property rights. The exception is the coverage under "nuisance and other regimes". Clearly other elements of delict provide redress against wrongful invasions of property rights; damage to or destruction of property may be seen as an interference with rights of ownership. Since the real right of ownership contains within it the right of use, damage to property may deprive the owner of that right and destruction usurps it entirely. Property damage may, of course, be the subject of an action for damages grounded on negligence. The law of neighbourhood is not, however, entirely concerned with ownership, but protects lesser rights incidental to ownership such as the right to exclusive possession (trespass and encroachment) or the right to comfortable enjoyment (nuisance).

NUISANCE

Nuisance protects the right of an occupier to the comfortable enjoyment **5–02** and use of heritable property, that is land or buildings. Such a right may be invaded by serious disturbance or substantial inconvenience, classically in the form of pollution of air by smoke or smells, pollution of water, unusual heat, noise or vibration. Interdict may be sought to end such disturbances whether in the forms just given or in any other form that amounts to a nuisance. Nuisance also grounds actions for damages usually in respect of physical damage to property caused, for example by withdrawal of support or flooding. It may help in understanding nuisance to consider it in terms of two overlapping categories. First the term "amenity nuisance" will be borrowed from academic literature on English law and used to describe intangible interferences with the use and enjoyment of property (like noise or smells) for which the primary remedy is interdict. Tangible physical damage to property will be considered separately. There is no legal division as such, this is purely a matter of presentation.

Amenity nuisance

Disturbing or inconvenient states of affairs affecting the occupier in their **5–03** premises or interfering with their use of land will amount to a legal wrong, but only if these can be established as a nuisance. Nobody can expect to live entirely free of such annoyances, the threshold for nuisance will only be reached when interference reaches a level deemed intolerable to the reasonable person in the circumstances. Nuisance then is a highly relative delict; it arises normally from activities that are perfectly lawful in themselves that become wrongful not simply because of their effect on others, but because of the extent of their effect, taking circumstances into account. No intent to injure on the part of the respondent is required. Indeed, the respondent may well act with clear conscience in the belief that the disturbance they cause is not sufficiently serious to warrant complaint. Equally, there is no need to show negligence. Where the complaint is of interference with amenity and no tangible (physical) damage is done, negligence will not provide a remedy. Negligence, moreover, will not serve to remedy distress or anxiety short of recognised psychiatric condition. Nuisance then, can provide a remedy in circumstances where negligence would not. *Culpa*, in any form, is not a requirement for the award of an interdict to restrain or abate nuisance.

The definitive statement of nuisance in Scots law is found in *Watt v Jamieson* in which Lord President Cooper took the unusual step of presiding over a case in the Outer House.

"[I]f any person so uses his property as to occasion serious disturbance or substantial inconvenience to his neighbour or material damage to his neighbour's property, it is in the general case irrelevant to plead merely that he was making a normal and familiar use of his own property. The balance in all such cases has to be held between the freedom of a proprietor to use his property as he pleases and the duty on a proprietor not to inflict material loss or inconvenience on adjoining proprietors and adjoining property; and in every case the answer depends on considerations of fact and degree ... The critical question is whether what he was exposed to was *plus quam tolerabile* when due weight has been given to all the surrounding circumstances of the offensive conduct and its effects."

This dictum introduced the *plus quam tolerabile* test for nuisance. *Plus quam tolerabile* simply means "more than tolerable" and may be referred to as the test of reasonable tolerability. A state of affairs becomes actionable as nuisance when interference exceeds the level of reasonable tolerability seen from the standpoint of the victim. The right of the respondent to use their property as they please is not an absolute right, it is relative and modified by the right of the petitioner to use their own. While the exercise of the respondent's right may impinge on the petitioner's right, if this goes too far there comes a tipping point and the respondent may be ordered to stop. In determining that tipping point, all relevant circumstances must be considered.

The circumstances to be taken into account will vary from case to case, but the one point that must always be established is the nature, extent and severity of the interference and its effects on the petitioner. The interference must be material—trivial interferences will not tip the balance. This point is expressed in a maxim: *lex non favet delicatorum votis* (the law does not consider the wishes of the fastidious). This raises the possibility of sensitivity of the petitioner as a circumstance that may work in favour of the defender if it can be established. In *Simpson v Miller* the occupant of an upper flat in an Edinburgh tenement failed to interdict the operation of a dough mixing machine in a baker's shop on the ground floor. In evidence it appeared that the vibration of which she complained was not experienced by any of the other occupants. It will be difficult to establish nuisance where interference affects a particularly sensitive land use or operation. In such cases there is some onus on the petitioner to take protective measures themselves to limit, reduce or obviate the disturbance. In *Armistead v Bowerman* the pursuer failed to obtain damages when fry in a fish hatchery were destroyed by silting of their pool as a result of the defender's logging operations upstream. The modification of the respondent's right to do as they please with or on their property does not extend to requiring them to take special account of the eccentric or unusual proclivities of the petitioner. The practicability of implementing remedial measures (which may amount to no more than shutting windows) is a circumstance that may be considered in relation to either party. If interference can easily be avoided by simple remedial measures on the part of the petitioner then a finding of nuisance is unlikely. On the other hand, the petitioner cannot be expected to remain indoors to avoid disturbances affecting the garden. It is not the case that there will be no finding of nuisance where it is simpler and cheaper for the victim to adopt remedial measures than it is for the respondent to abate, although depending on other considerations, that is a possible result.

The suitability of the land use or operation complained of to the locality also may be a relevant circumstance as indeed may the suitability of the use to be protected. What ought to be tolerated in one place may be intolerable elsewhere. In *Maguire v Charles McNeil Ltd* the Archbishop of Glasgow and others failed to interdict the use of drop hammers in a forge. He was resident in a district in which there was much heavy industry. The suitability of the use complained of to the locality weighed in the respondent's favour in this case. Even so, the court affirmed that the existence of a level of disturbance which must be tolerated does not entitle anyone to make a material increase.

Materiality must be established in evidence, so for example a complaint of noise should be supported by measurements. Noise disturbance, however, is not always simply a matter of volume; its nature may also be relevant. A level of noise that would otherwise be within the bounds of tolerability may be more disturbing, and therefore a nuisance where persons are subjected in their homes to the sound of animals being dispatched in a slaughterhouse (*Kelt v Lindsay*). Equally, time is relevant so bell ringing might be tolerable during the day but a different matter in the middle of the night. The same might be said of piano or guitar playing. People can reasonably be expected to put up with temporary disturbances, but duration may make the difference. In *The Globe (Aberdeen) Ltd v North of Scotland Water Authority* the complaint concerned road works scheduled to last six weeks that had continued over nine months. This had created mess, muddy pavements in particular rendering access to the pub both inconvenient and unattractive and leading to loss of business.

Defences
Defences must be distinguished from factors taken into account in the **5–04** process of applying the *plus quam tolerabile* test. A defence, if established, will override a finding of nuisance.

Statutory authority for the operation complained of may provide a defence, but only where nuisance is the inevitable outcome of the operation, irrespective of measures that may be taken to effect abatement. The defender may be called upon to show that all care has been taken and, if this is established, then nuisance will be regarded as the inevitable outcome and the defence will hold.

Acquiescence affords a defence equivalent to volenti non fit injuria in other areas of delict. Volenti does not appear to apply since the rule is that it is no defence that the complainer came to the nuisance (see, for example, *Fleming v Hislop* and *Webster v Lord Advocate*).

For acquiescence to succeed as a defence it is necessary to show that the petitioner had full knowledge of and consented, not merely to the activity complained of, but also to the harm or disturbance. This consent must be shown by something more positive than silence or a failure to object, although tolerance of the situation over a long period of time will point towards acquiescence. Acquiescence will not preclude an action where there is a material increase in the level of disturbance or harm.

Contributory fault has no role to play in nuisance. The Law Reform (Contributory Negligence) Act 1945 does not apply. Any role played by the petitioner, for example a failure to take simple remedial measures, may be taken into account in balancing the interests of the parties.

It is not possible to acquire a prescriptive right to create a nuisance. On the other hand, the right to object to nuisance may be lost after 20 years under s.8 of the Prescription and Limitation (Scotland) Act 1973. The right to reparation will be lost after five years by virtue of s.6 on the basis that the obligation arises not from land, but from fault. The prescriptive period does not begin to run from the start of the offensive operation, but from the point at which it amounts to nuisance.

Interdict

5–05 When nuisance is established an interdict may be awarded. The terms of interdict should be framed no wider than necessary to obviate the nuisance. Any restriction placed on the respondent's right should be kept to a minimum so that activities or operations will not necessarily be ordered to stop if remedial measures can be implemented so they can be carried on without giving rise to nuisance. Public interest moreover cannot over-ride private right. The Court of Session does, however, have power to suspend an interdict when, in the words of Lord McLaren in *Clippens Oil Co v Edinburgh & District Water Trustees*:

> "[T]he granting of immediate interdict would be attended with consequences to the rights of the respondents as injurious, or possibly more so, than the wrong that was complained of or ... because the effect of an immediate interdict would be to cause some great and immediate public inconvenience."

Before the power to suspend interdict is exercised, it is necessary first to reach a finding on the facts. In this way the consequences for defenders and the public interest will already have been taken into account in the process of determining whether the interference is more than reasonably tolerable, bearing in mind that tolerability is assessed from the standpoint of the victim. An overwhelming public interest in an operation will not prevent a finding of nuisance if the interference is severe. In such circumstances interdict may be suspended in order to allow time for remedial measures to be put in place. In *Ben Nevis Distillery (Fort William) Ltd v The North British Aluminium Co Ltd* the operation that the petitioners sought to have interdicted involved 72 per cent of UK aluminium production and a significant number of jobs. Fumes from the operation were affecting air quality, pure air being vital in the production of quality malt whisky. In this case interdict was awarded, but its operation was suspended to allow the defenders to implement remedial measures. A similar result was achieved in *Webster v Lord Advocate*, in which a resident just down from the castle esplanade found the noise from preparations for the Edinburgh Tattoo intolerable.

While discussion so far has focussed on ending states of affairs that amount to nuisance, interdict may also be sought prospectively to prevent an operation or conduct that will certainly give rise to nuisance if carried out. This may be seen for example in the House of Lords case *Fleming v Hislop* upholding an interdict awarded to prevent disposal of pit bings by firing them, a proposal which would have affected the residents in neighbouring properties for years as the bings smouldered slowly away. In *Cumnock and Doon Valley District Council v Dance Energy Associates Ltd* a rave was interdicted on grounds of anticipated noise disturbance. Prospective and present dangers, such as fire hazards, may be interdicted in nuisance as occurred in *Vary v Thomson*. Interdict was granted against a blacksmith's operation in the vicinity of thatched houses. It remains the case that a dangerous state of affairs may be the subject of a court order. In *Canmore Housing Association v Bairnsfather* the petitioner was unable to obtain an interim remedy under s.47(2) of the Court of Session Act 1988. The petitioner sought to have the respondent ordered to remove derelict cars parked against its property, but failed because it could not be established that the risk of harm was material. Where a material risk of material harm is established then a remedy ought to be available.

Damages
Unlike in England the court has no power to refuse interdict and make an **5–06** award of damages in lieu. Awards of damages must be concluded for, that is specifically requested in pleadings. The fact that interdict is the primary remedy in amenity nuisance does not mean that damages claims are restricted to cases of tangible physical harm. Damages may be sought, for example, where the harm or interference is completed, in which case interdict would be pointless and, in any event unavailable since interdicts will not be granted without a reasonable prospect of a repeated or continuing wrong. Equally, damages may be sought where abatement of the nuisance is impossible. This was the case in *Chalmers v Dixon*. This case will also serve to illustrate the point that a source of amenity harm, that is inconvenience or disturbance, may give rise also to more tangible losses for which reparation will likely be sought. The case was brought by a farmer against neighbouring proprietors on whose property was a bing that had somehow caught light. Not only did the resultant smoke make life in

the farmhouse intolerable, but it affected the health of the pursuer and his family and damaged crops. Another example is found in *Shanlin v Collins*. In that case a husband and wife sought interdict and damages against a neighbour whose dogs created sufficient disturbance to prevent the couple from sleeping. An interdict was granted and damages were awarded the wife in respect of the nervous debility she developed as a consequence of sleep deprivation and the general state of affairs. Both cases demonstrate the possibility of reparation for damage to health in actions grounded in nuisance. Nuisance also may support claims for economic losses, although, as in the case of injury to health, the case law is somewhat sparse. *The Globe (Aberdeen) Ltd v NWSA* was mentioned earlier. In a later case brought against the same defender, *Hand v NSWA* damages were sought in respect of business losses incurred by the Ladywell Tavern in Dundee following flooding of the premises by operations carried out behind the pub. In *Black Loch Angling Club v Tarmac Ltd* the pursuers recovered losses on sales of fishing permits following silting of the water by the defenders.

This brings discussion to the point where tangible physical harm cases can be considered. The coverage up to here has involved ongoing states of affairs or anticipated events susceptible of interdict and readily characterised in terms of nuisance. It has been noted also how such circumstances can give rise to claims for damages. When, however, discussion moves to consider actions for damages where the complaint is of tangible physical harm to heritable property, it is found that actions may arise, not solely from on-going disturbing or inconvenient states of affairs, but also from one-off events. Later case law includes, for instance, flooding of premises due to a burst sewer (*RHM Bakeries (Scotland) Ltd v Strathclyde Regional Council*) or to blocked or inadequate culverts (*GA Estates Ltd v Caviapen Trustees Ltd*, *Viewpoint Housing Association v Edinburgh City Council*). Actions may also arise from withdrawal of support (*Reo Stakis Organisation v Strathclyde Regional Council, Kennedy v Glenbelle, Hamilton v Wahla*) or from operations leaving gable ends exposed to the elements (*Powrie v Dundee City Council*; *Morris Amusements Ltd v Glasgow City Council*). Equally, actions still arise from circumstances more traditionally recognisable as nuisance such as water pollution (*Black Loch Angling Club v Tarmac Ltd*; *Esso Petroleum v Scottish Ministers*) and noise (*King v Advocate General for Scotland*).

When damages are sought it is by no means clear that the *plus quam tolerabile* test is applied in every case, although Lord President Hope did stipulate in *Kennedy v Glenbelle* that nuisance must first be established. Indeed, the test was clearly considered essential in the Outer House case *Chalmers v Diageo Scotland Ltd* in which the pursuers complained that ethanol fumes emanating from the defenders' premises had generated the growth of fungus on their home. Harm of course must be established in any case, but the need to balance the interests of the parties where there is structural or flood damage to the pursuer's property is not immediately apparent. It may be noted that actions where the harm was flooding or withdrawal of support were not brought in nuisance before the latter half of the 20th century and exposure of gable ends as nuisance appears to be an innovation of the 21st. The extent to which such cases are fully accommodated within the theory of the doctrine may be questionable.

Culpa

The critical difference between actions for interdict and actions for damages **5–07** is that *culpa* must be averred and proved for the latter. The requirement for *culpa* was established by Lord Fraser in the House of Lords in *RHM Bakeries (Scotland) Ltd v Strathclyde Regional Council* in 1985. In that case the pursuer's premises had been flooded by a burst sewer for which the defender was responsible. Without averments of fault the action failed. Before *RHM* there had been a strong body of opinion supported, albeit not unambiguously, by authority to the effect that liability in nuisance was strict. The next major development on the exposition of *culpa* in nuisance was delivered in the Inner House in *Kennedy v Glenbelle*. The model of *culpa* proposed by Lord President Hope has been covered above in the introductory chapter. In *Kennedy* it was held that an averment of a deliberate act, done in the knowledge that harm would be the likely result, was a sufficient averment of *culpa* to go to proof. Liability, then, is based on intention. Subsequently it has been determined, in *GB & AM Anderson v White*, that the necessary knowledge may be established constructively. The issue is not what the defender actually knew, but what ought to have been apparent to a reasonable person in the position of the defender. The judgment in *Kennedy* has been taken to indicate that nuisance is a delict of intention and that when harm is caused negligently the ordinary principles of negligence should apply. In the context of damages, however, it is probably safer to say that the relationship between nuisance and negligence remains a little unclear. Certainly, it is not uncommon to see alternative pleas of intentional fault and negligence in the same case, *Kennedy* itself was one such, and, moreover, recognition of a duty of care is unlikely to prove a major obstacle in most instances. Judicial discussion on the difference between intention and negligence in nuisance may be found in *Cunningham v Cameron*.

There has, arguably, been something of a recurring theme in nuisance that requirements for liability should not place an undue burden on pursuers. This is indeed evident in the present formulation of intentional liability based on constructive knowledge. The same concern was expressed earlier by Lord Fraser in *RHM* when he stated:

"As a general rule it would, in my opinion, be relevant for a pursuer to make averments to the effect that his property has been damaged by a flood caused by an event on the defender's land, such as the collapse of sewer which it was the defender's duty to maintain, that properly maintained sewers do not collapse, and that the collapse is evidence that the defender had failed in his duty to maintain the sewer. The onus will then be on the defender to explain the event in some way consistent with absence of fault on his part."

Three years later averments of fault drafted along these lines were held irrelevant in *Argyll and Clyde Health Board v Strathclyde Regional Council*. This was because the substance of the case was that the defenders had failed to maintain a water pipe; in short, the allegation concerned negligence. Without averments on what a proper maintenance regime would involve the pursuers had failed to specify the standard of care and so the defenders were not given the notice to which they were entitled of the case against them. This was a case of negligence masquerading as nuisance. Lord Fraser's dictum did, however, find its application in 2016 in Airdrie sheriff appeal court. *McKenna v O'Hare* was brought against a neighbour from whose property a quantity of kerosene had leaked, causing sufficient damage to two houses to require their demolition and rebuilding. Pleadings in the form suggested by Lord Fraser were held effective in circumstances where it proved impossible at proof to determine whether the leak occurred when the oil tank containing the kerosene was moved, which would have been negligence, or whether the kerosene was deliberately poured onto the ground from a container, which would have been an intentional act. Either way, it was clear that the leak originated with the defender and that he was responsible.

Nuisance and other regimes

5–08 Aside from the common law other regimes play a role in regulating nuisance or, like planning, operate to limit the scope for nuisance arising. Planning permission will not be forthcoming, for example, for industrial land uses in a residential area. Many of the complaints litigated during the late 18th and throughout the 19th centuries, when people did set up industrial process in their own back yards or operated steam engines in tenement flats *(Johnston v Constable)*, would simply not occur in the modern context. Uses of land may also be regulated through real burdens. It was for a long time more or less standard in the urban environment to inhibit any uses which would give rise to nuisance by means of real burdens. Such restrictions may still be imposed in title conditions and may be made a term of a lease. There are a number of regulatory provisions scattered around administrative and, indeed, criminal law that have a bearing on nuisance. If, for example, a neighbour is giving reasonable cause for annoyance they may be ordered by a police officer to desist. Failure to do so is an offence under s.54(1) of the Civil Government (Scotland) Act 1982. Local authorities have various powers to deal with nuisances, the most obviously relevant of which are found in the Environmental Protection Act 1990. The term "statutory nuisance" is normally taken to refer to this particular body of law. These provisions ultimately derive from the Public Health (Scotland) Act of 1867, though they have been through various incarnations since, most recent amendments being made by the Public Health (Scotland) Act 2008. The public health legislation of the 19th century was enacted because of the inability of the common law and local neighbourhood regulation to deal effectively with sanitation and matters of public health in expanding urban communities. These concerns were prompted especially by a number of cholera epidemics. Statutory nuisance belongs in public and administrative law rather than delict, but its relevance here should be obvious. Clearly if the source of annoyance is covered by the legislation it is easier to complain to the local authority than it is to initiate civil litigation. That said, the common law may provide a remedy where the local authority fails to act or indeed is the source of the disturbance.

Section 79(1) of the Environmental Protection Act 1990 lists statutory nuisances as follows:

(a) any premises in such a state as to be prejudicial to health or a nuisance;

(b) smoke emitted from premises so as to be prejudicial to health or a nuisance;

(c) fumes or gases emitted from premises so as to be prejudicial to health or a nuisance;

(d) any dust, steam, smell or other effluvia arising on industrial trade or business premises so as to be prejudicial to health or a nuisance;

(e) any accumulation or deposit which is prejudicial to health or a nuisance;

(ea) any water covering land or land covered with water which is in such a state as to be prejudicial to health or a nuisance;

(f) any animal kept in such a place or manner as to be prejudicial to health or a nuisance;

(faa) any insects emanating from premises and being prejudicial to health or a nuisance;

(fba) artificial light emitted from:
   (i) premises;
   (ii) any stationary object,
so as to be prejudicial to health or a nuisance;

(g) noise emitted from premises so as to be prejudicial to health or a nuisance;

(ga) noise that is prejudicial to health or a nuisance and is emitted from or caused by a vehicle, machinery or equipment in a street or in Scotland, road;

(h) any other matter declared by any enactment to be a statutory nuisance.

Each local authority is under a duty to detect statutory nuisances and, where complaints are brought, to take reasonable steps to investigate. Where statutory nuisance is found, the authority is obliged under s.80 to issue a notice to ensure that the nuisance is abated. Those on whom the abatement notice is served have a right of appeal to the sheriff court. Contravention of an abatement notice constitutes a criminal offence (s.80(4)). Liability to conviction may be discharged on payment of a fixed penalty (s.80(4A)). Section 82 allows for direct application to the sheriff court by individuals.

USE OF LAND *IN AEMULATIONEM VICINI*

5–09 This delict pre-dates nuisance in the common law. Complaints by neighbours could be met by the argument that proprietors could do as they wished on their property so long as they were not restrained by servitude and did not act *in aemulationem*. Technically, this means acting out of spite. Under the doctrine of *aemulationem vicini* the pursuer must aver and prove malice. In order for malice to be inferred, it must be clear that the predominant purpose of the activity complained of was to harm or annoy. Therefore, if the defender can establish that the offensive act was conducted for their own convenience or benefit and that harm to the pursuer was merely consequential, then an action *in aemulationem* will be defeated. The action can be defended where the operation or activity that is the subject of complaint is conducted, or situated where it is for the convenience of the defender. In *Dewar v Fraser* the pursuer, Fraser, failed to prevent his neighbour from erecting two lime kilns on the part of his property nearest to Fraser's own, anticipating that his holiday home would be rendered uninhabitable by smoke when the wind was in the west. Dewar maintained that his chosen location was the one most convenient to himself. This case came before the Court in 1767, before the doctrine of nuisance had fully taken root in the common law. By contrast, in the following year a Glasgow surgeon, William Ralston succeed in having a brick kiln removed from his neighbour's garden despite the clear convenience of its location next to the clay pit. *Ralston v Pettigrew* can be distinguished from *Dewar* on the basis that smoke had done actual damage to Ralston's trees and plants, but it is notable that the issue of nuisance was raised as a further limitation on rights of land use.

The volume of subsequent case law on *aemulationem vicini* is extremely limited. In *Campbell v Muir* petitioner and respondent were neighbouring proprietors on opposite banks of the river Awe. The respondent moored his boat in the middle of the river and cast his rod in such a way as to prevent Sir Robert Usher, who had leased the fishing rights from the petitioner, from continuing to fish. Sir Robert had been fishing at that spot for five minutes before the arrival of Muir. The pool where the men were fishing was some 60 yards wide by 146 yards long. Therefore, there was plenty of space for Muir to fish the pool without interfering with Sir Robert. The case *in aemulationem* was established. In *More v Boyle* the defender severed a water connection in his back garden in order to "get his own back" on neighbours who had refused to pay for a repair on the water pipe. The case *in aemulationem* was held relevant.

While *aemulationem* remains part of the common law, its utility in the modern law may be regarded as doubtful. Spiteful conduct by neighbours may be more easily remedied under the Protection from Harassment Act.

SUPPORT

Withdrawal of support is an interference with a property right giving rise **5–10** to a claim for damages. Support may be subjacent or adjacent. The support given land by the substrata is subjacent as is the support given upper properties by lower where ownership is divided horizontally as in tenements. Adjacent support refers to support from neighbouring properties, i.e. next door. The Tenements (Scotland) Act s.11 imposes on lower proprietors a duty to support upper levels. Liability for withdrawal of subjacent support within buildings depends on *culpa* (*Thomson v St Cuthbert's Co-operative Association Ltd; Kennedy v Glenbelle*). Subjacent support to land may be withdrawn by the excavation of minerals beneath the surface, bearing in mind that the owner of the land and the party with the right to extract minerals from beneath the land are not necessarily the same person. Where the mineral extracted is coal, compensation is regulated by the Coal Industry Act 1994. When a large void appeared in their property and the house had to be evacuated and then demolished, a couple received compensation under s.10 of the Water (Scotland) Act as the sinkhole had been caused by a burst water main (*O'Connor and Docherty v Scottish Water*). Otherwise, where subsidence or any other damage is done to land by withdrawal of subjacent support, liability at common law is strict. In *Angus v NCB* Lord Justice-clerk Thomson stated:

"The right of support is an incident of property. The owner, in virtue of his ownership, has the right to have his land left in its natural state and he enjoys that right *qua* owner. If the owner's right of support is breached, he becomes entitled to damages for surface damage without requiring to establish negligence."

Liability for withdrawal of adjacent support to land is strict. The ability of a proprietor to excavate property right up to the boundary depends on the nature of the substrata. The exception is where buildings are joined by a common gable built on the boundary. In these circumstances, liability for withdrawal of support is based on *culpa*. A proprietor has no right to take support from a gable built entirely on the neighbour's side of the boundary without a servitude right to do so.

It has already been seen that withdrawal of support cases have been grounded on nuisance. Whether this has been a useful development is open to question. While some cases have been grounded in nuisance, there are other analogous cases which have proceeded with no reference to nuisance, such as *GUS Property Management v Littlewoods Mail Order Stores, Stewart v Malik* and *K2 Restaurants v Glasgow City Council*. The position is summarised accurately by Niall Whitty as follows, "[t]he relationship between nuisance and rights of support ... is uncertain and confused" ("Nuisance" in *Stair Memorial Encyclopaedia* (2001) para.29).

TRESPASS AND RELATED DELICTS

5–11 Trespass is concerned with temporary and unjustifiable intrusions onto heritable property. The interest protected is the right to exclusive use and possession. Permanent physical intrusions, such as walls, overhanging eaves or even branches are not trespass, but encroachment (see, e.g. *Halkerston v Wedderburn*). As Guthrie-Smith wrote in 1864, "[a]n owner of real property must carefully confine himself and his operations within his own boundary. His erections must not project on his neighbour's ground, nor his trees overhang the intervening wall". Squatting is not trespass but intrusion. Intrusion operates where the owner is not in possession at the time. Where the owner is ejected from the property this is yet another delict, ejection.

Heritable property is owned *a coelo usque ad centrum*, that is "from the sky to the centre of the earth", so air space above the property is protected against trespass and encroachment. However, trespass may not be mobilised against over-flying aircraft by virtue of the Civil Aviation Act 1982 s.2. Trespass on moveable property that may be occupied, such as ships or oil rigs, is actionable (see *Phestos Shipping Co Ltd v Kurmiawan* and *Shell UK Ltd v McGillivray*).

While damages are available in respect of tangible harm done, for example, to crops, the primary remedy against trespass is interdict. Interdict may be refused, for example, because of the triviality of the invasion complained of. The most famous case is *Winans v MacRae* in which the owner of 200,000 acres of deer forest was refused interdict to prevent a pet lamb from straying onto his land. For an award of interdict there must be reasonable apprehension that future trespass will occur (see, e.g. *Hay's Trustees v Young*). Interdict is personal and is only effective against persons named on the petition. An interdict against one person will not be effective against another who is not named. Interdict may be effective in cases of sit-ins in industrial disputes. For example, in *Caterpillar (UK) Ltd* interdict was granted against 808 named individuals. In other circumstances it may be impossible to identify the relevant individuals (see, for example, *Stirling Crawfurd v Clyde Navigation Trustees*). It has been observed that interdict in trespass is only truly effective against persistent identifiable individuals. While proprietors can take precautionary measures to protect their privacy the use of force is likely to give rise to liability in assault.

The most important common law defence to trespass is justification. By definition, a trespass is an unjustifiable intrusion so where there is justification there is no trespass. It is accepted, for instance, that there is no trespass where land is entered to apprehend a criminal or to fight a fire. Furthermore, there are many instances in which entering land is authorised by statute. Acquiescence also provides a defence. Consent to enter land may be express or implied, but consent, once given, can always be withdrawn (see, for example, *Steuart v Stephen* and *Love-Lee v Cameron of Locheil*).

The most significant development in the law has been the coming into force of Statutory Access Rights under the Land Reform (Scotland) Act 2003. Section 1 provides everybody with two distinct rights. One is the right to be on land for specified purposes of recreation, educational activities or commercial enterprises. The other is the right to cross land. These rights only exist to the extent that they are exercised responsibly (s.2) and there are various exclusions and restrictions (see ss.6, 7 and 9). This development leaves two regimes in place, the relationship between them is not entirely clear, though it is not apparent that this has caused any major problem. Where land is accessed under the statutory rights, regulation falls under the Act, s.28 of which empowers the sheriff court to determine questions of access and responsibility. Scope remains, however, for trespass where there is no question of statutory rights and so the relevance of the common law continues.

6. PARTICULAR REGIMES

6–01 There is no real linking theme to the topics covered in this chapter. They are certainly not linked by any common requirement for liability. Occupiers' liability, liability for harm done by animals and product liability are all forms of statutory delict with the first requiring negligence and strict liability being imposed in the latter two. The common law continues to operate in addition in all three areas of law. Fraud, passing off and the economic delicts are delicts of intention governed by the common law. The topics are presented together purely for convenience.

OCCUPIERS' LIABILITY

6–02 The governing statute is the Occupiers' Liability (Scotland) Act 1960, s.2(1) of which imposes a duty of care on the occupiers of land or premises in the following terms:

> "The care which an occupier of premises is required, by reason of his occupation or control of the premises, to show towards a person entering thereon in respect of dangers which are due to the state of the premises or to anything done or omitted to be done on them and for which the occupier is in law responsible shall, except in so far as he is entitled to and does restrict, modify or exclude by agreement his obligations towards that person, be such care as in all the circumstances of the case is reasonable to see that that person will not suffer injury or damage by reason of any such danger."

The first point of note is that this duty is not restricted to heritable property, but extends also to include "any fixed or moveable structure, including any vessel, vehicle or aircraft, and to persons entering thereon" (s.1(3)(a)). The second is that the duty is not restricted to private property, but covers public spaces as well. The third is that the duty is imposed on the party in occupation or control. In the case of public spaces this is likely to be the local authority. Where the body responsible is in doubt, s.1(2) provides that identification of the correct party is a matter for the common law. Where property is let, s.3 provides that the duty may fall on the landlord, but only in respect of sources of harm for which they are responsible under the terms of the lease. The duty will not fall on the owner if another party is in control, for example where a house has been vacated and left in the control of builders.

> "The party in control is the person who has the right and means in the circumstances of taking effective steps to protect the visitor from the particular danger whether by removal, notice, fencing or forbidding

entry to the premises" (Gloag and Henderson, *The Law of Scotland*, 14th edn (Edinburgh: W. Green, 2017) para.27.04).

In *Dawson v Page* a homeowner had vacated her house while building work was carried out, but as she returned to the house every day it was held that she had not relinquished control and so was held to owe a duty to the pursuer albeit the duty was not breached in that case.

The duty is owed to persons entering the property irrespective of their purpose for being there. The duty is to take reasonable care in the circumstances. The standard of care is therefore variable according to the relevant circumstances that include the conditions on which the pursuer is present, the nature of the source of harm and the known or foreseeable characteristics of the person to whom the duty is owed. As Lord Reid stated in the House of Lords in *McGlone v British Railways Board*:

> "The section applies both to trespassers and to persons entering property by invitation or licence express or implied. But that does not mean that the occupier must always show equal care for the safety of all such persons ... In deciding what degree of care is required ... regard must be had both to the position of the occupier and to the position of the person entering his premises and it may often be reasonable to hold that an occupier must do more to protect a person whom he permits to be on his property than he need do to protect a person who enters the property without permission." (*McGlone v B.R.B.*, 1966 S.L.T. 2 at 9, per Lord Reid, HL.)

McGlone concerned a 12-year-old boy who had been burnt by a transformer. The defenders were held to have acted reasonably, that is they had fulfilled their duty of care in erecting a fence and posting warning signs. It would not have been possible to have reached the danger without expending considerable effort.

The susceptibility of the standard of care to variations in circumstances means that occupiers' liability cases tend to be highly fact specific. Each case does not, however, turn entirely on its own facts and some general observations may be made. As noted, the characteristics of the pursuer are relevant and the standard of care may be more exacting in respect of persons particularly vulnerable to hazards, for example the visually impaired or young children. In *Taylor v Glasgow Corporation* the defenders were liable when a seven-year-old boy ate the berries of atropa belladonna (deadly nightshade), a shrub planted in a part of a public park in which children were known to play. The shrub was a danger due to the state of the premises and no precautions had been taken or warnings given. A further point pertinent to this case is that some dangers are liable to attract children, making harm all the more foreseeable and raising the degree of care needed. In *Anderson v Imrie* an eight-year-old boy incurred skull and brain injuries when a heavy gate on which he was climbing fell, knocking his head against the concrete floor. The occupier of the farm where the injury occurred had undertaken to look after the boy as he played with her own son and she had left the boys to their own devices as she groomed a horse. It was held that she ought to have foreseen the attraction of the gate to the boy and should have taken care to prevent access to that part of the farm. Moreover, she had allowed the boy out of her sight and beyond her supervision for an unreasonably long time.

6–03   The duty is owed specifically in respect of dangers due to the state of the premises or to things done or omitted to be done on them. It can be seen that the Act imposes a positive duty to act and a failure to do so will likely be a breach, so liability for omissions, normally exceptional in the context of negligence, is an inherent and commonly occurring feature of the law on occupiers' liability. That said, the burden falls on the pursuer to establish the action that the defender ought to have taken and didn't. It may be noted in passing that an aggressive nightclub bouncer is not a danger within the meaning of the Act (*Honeybourne v Burgess*). As a general point it may be said that there is no duty to guard against obvious dangers. The *locus classicus* is *Stevenson v Glasgow Corporation*, an action brought by the father of a young child who had fallen into the River Kelvin and drowned. In rejecting the case Lord McLaren drew attention to the sheer impracticability of fencing off rivers. The law on this point has been summed up more recently by Lord Johnston in *Fegan v Highland Regional Council*, an action brought by a woman who had survived a fall from a cliff at Thurso.

> "In general terms an occupier of land containing natural phenomena such as rivers or cliffs, which present obvious dangers, is not required to take precautions against persons becoming injured by reason of those dangers unless there are special risks such as unusual or unseen sources of danger."

The simple fact that a feature is man-made does not mean that it should be regarded any differently from the rivers and cliffs to which Lord Johnstone referred if the danger is obvious. Thus, no duty arose in respect of a reservoir in which a farmer drowned (*Graham v East of Scotland Water Authority*). The fact that a danger is "obvious", however, is not in itself decisive without considering other relevant circumstances. What is obvious in daylight may not be so in the dark and what can clearly be seen from one direction may be hidden when approached from another. These were relevant circumstances in *Cowan v Hopetoun House Preservation Trust* (discussed below).

The occupier must implement reasonable measures to guard against dangers by fencing them off, effecting repairs, giving warnings, such as prohibiting access or requiring small children to be accompanied, or whatever is appropriate in the circumstances. Visitors are of course expected to take some responsibility for their own safety and very small children need looking after. The defence of volenti non fit injuria is preserved in the Act in s.2(3), meaning that the occupier has a complete defence if it can be shown that the pursuer knowingly assented to run the risk of injury. This defence has been applied in a number of cases, but where the victim is a child the issue of their ability to appreciate the risk arises. In *Titchener v British Railways Board* an action was brought by a 15-year-old girl who had been seriously injured while crossing a railway line. Her boyfriend was killed in the incident. The argument that the defender had been negligent in failing to maintain a fence made of sleepers—some sleepers were missing so there were gaps—was defeated. It was held that at 15 the pursuer would have appreciated the danger posed by trains. The 14-year-old victim in *Devlin v Strathclyde Regional Council* was playing tig on a school roof when he decided to bounce off a skylight window from a height of some five feet in order to evade capture. The flaw in this plan became evident as he crashed through the skylight to his death. Had the defender been in breach—again the boy was trespassing and had had to overcome obstacles in getting onto the roof—volenti would have applied.

Findings of contributory negligence are common in occupiers' liability cases. In *McLeod v British Railways Board* a 12-year-old boy fell on power cables carrying 25,000 volts. He spent nine months in hospital and underwent 10 skin graft operations. The defender was found liable with a 20 per cent reduction in damages for contributory negligence. In *Cowan v Hopetoun House Preservation Trust* damages were reduced by 75 per cent when a 61-year-old man fell five feet into the ha-ha (a ditch or drop in level of a type used on large properties to border lawns without interrupting views) and broke his ankle. The incident occurred in the dark, the pursuer had been on a guided "bat walk" on the estate with his grandson and the defenders' employee could reasonably have done a little more to have warned visitors of the danger. Nevertheless, it was established that the pursuer was not paying close enough attention to where he was going. The damages awarded in *Anderson v Imrie* were reduced by 25 per cent to reflect the child's own fault.

It may be recalled that s.2(1) allows for restriction, modification or exclusion of the duty by agreement. Any such attempt will, however, be subject to provisions in the Consumer Rights Act 2015 where it applies or to those in the Unfair Contract Terms Act 1977. The former statute will apply in most cases where the visitor is a customer of a business entering land under a contract to do so, for example when using a car park, going to a club, visiting a castle or gardens or a zoo. Equally, the Act will apply whenever the relation between the parties is one of consumer and trader for example in a pub or shop. Section 65(1) provides that a trader cannot, by a term of a consumer contract or by a consumer notice, exclude or restrict liability for death or personal injury resulting from negligence. Section 65(4) applies the above provision explicitly to the duty under the 1960 Act. When the relationship between the parties is not that of consumer and trader, where for example a plumber is on business premises servicing the boiler, s.16 of the Unfair Contract Terms Act has a similar effect. There is a slightly curious exception in the 2015 Act. Section 66(4) dis-applies s.65 in the case where persons accessing premises for recreational purposes are injured because of their dangerous state. The provision only operates where "allowing the person access for those purposes is not within the purposes of the occupier's trade, business, craft or profession". The scope for this must be fairly limited. The operators of a soft play area for instance could not restrict, modify or exclude their duty even when admitting children—or indeed adults—without charge since recreation is their business. Section 66(4) might come into play if, for example, the occupier of a slaughterhouse acceding to a request to use the premises for skateboarding when empty of animals, agreed on the understanding that boarders use the premises entirely at their own risk.

LIABILITY FOR ANIMALS

6–04 Where damage to person or property is done by animals, liability may arise either at common law or under the Animals (Scotland) Act 1987. The preferable route for the pursuer is to sue under the Act since liability is strict, whereas liability at common law is dependent on establishing *culpa* on the part of the owner. Normally this will entail proof of negligence, but if the act complained of involves intention, for example if a dog has been deliberately set to attack then *culpa* may be established on that basis. In order to base an action on the Act it is first necessary to establish that the Act applies in the circumstances. The Act applies to two types of damage caused by two different classes of animal. It covers personal injury and death caused by fierce animals in the course of an attack, whether the victim is human or another animal. What amounts to an attack includes savaging or harrying, but boisterous or clumsy behaviour is not an attack. Actions brought under the Act where pursuers have been knocked over by frisky dogs have failed (see *Fairley v Carruthers* [Golden Retriever] and *Welsh v Brady* [Black Labrador]). Injury includes causing a pregnant animal to abort, any diminution in the produce of an animal and any disease sustained as the consequence of an attack, but does not include simple contagion of disease such as the spread of bovine tuberculosis from one herd of cows to another (see ss.7 and s.1(4)). The Act also covers property damage done by foraging animals, that is those likely to cause material property damage in the course of foraging. The statutory language does not designate animals as fierce or foraging as such, but this division summarises the effect of the provisions. The party liable under the Act is the keeper of the animal (s.1(1)(a)). In most cases the keeper will be the owner, but other possibilities are provided for in s.5. For example, where the animal is owned by a child under 16 years of age the keeper is the person with actual care and control of the child; where an animal has escaped or been abandoned, the keeper is the person who was owner or had the animal in their possession at the time of escape or abandonment. This raises the point that possession of the animal without being owner may be sufficient to make a person keeper. Possession is not defined in the Act, but it seems likely that where, for example a dog attacks while being exercised by a dog-walker, the dog-walker rather than the owner would be the keeper.

Faced with a potential claim under the Act the first task is to identify the defender, that is the keeper. Next, the question whether the animal is one covered by the Act needs to be ascertained. Animals deemed likely to cause property damage by foraging are helpfully listed in s.1(3) as "cattle, horses, asses, mules, hinnies, sheep, pigs, goats and deer". Other than dogs, which are specifically named, there is a bit of a trail to be followed to determine whether a particular animal is fierce, that is one deemed likely to attack. Section 1(3) refers the reader to s.7(4) of the Dangerous Wild Animals Act 1976, which in turn refers to those animals listed in the Schedule to the Act. This provides a long list of such animals including the obvious candidates: wolves, lions, tigers, crocodiles, buthid scorpions and walrus; the exotic: hog badger, hairy-nosed otter and pronghorn; and the surprising: giant anteaters are perhaps not as cuddly as might have been thought. If the animal is not one listed, then evidence will have to be led to satisfy the court that, "the animal belongs to a species whose members generally are by virtue of their physical attributes and habits likely (unless controlled or restrained) to injure severely or kill persons or animals, or damage property to a material extent", depending on the form of harm sustained (s.1(1)(b)). In *Foskett v McClymont* the question whether a bull is a species liable to injure was allowed to go to proof. This was a question of fact to be demonstrated by appropriate evidence. Viruses, bacteria, algae, fungi and protozoa are specifically excluded under s.7. According to accepted taxonomy, none of these are, in any sense, animals. Also, s.1(5) excludes liability under the Act where injury or damage is caused by the mere fact that the animal is "present on a road or in any other place". Given that the Act only covers injuries caused by an attack or property damage caused by foraging, this provision might be though to be otiose. Nevertheless, there is case law on the point, e.g. *Bennett v Lamont and Sons* in which a driver and passenger were injured when swerving to avoid cows which had strayed onto the road. Both the action under the Act and the common law case failed, the latter because fault on the part of the defenders could not be shown.

Liability under the Act is strict, it is not absolute so there is a number of defences provided for by s.2. No liability arises under the Act if the harm sustained was wholly due to the fault of the victim or the keeper of another animal where that animal is the victim. In cases where injury is partially the fault of the victim, a reduction in damages for contributory negligence is competent. In *Ferguson v Ferguson* the jury found the pursuer 85 per cent to blame for a bite she sustained when she frightened a pet dog by sticking her face up against its and pulling its cheeks. The defence of volenti non fit injuria is also available. Section 2(1)(c) provides a defence where a person or animal is injured when present on the keeper's land without authority, in short while trespassing. However, where the animal causing the injury is on the land "wholly or partly for the purposes of protecting persons or property" then the s.2(1)(c) defence is disapplied by s.2(2). In these circumstances the defence will be lost and liability will be strict unless the use made of the guard animal was reasonable and, where the animal is a guard dog, s.1 of the Guard Dogs Act 1975 must have been complied with. This provision requires guard dogs to be under the control of their handlers or secured so that they cannot roam freely about the premises. Additionally, warning notices must be exhibited at every entrance to the premises.

Where the Act does not apply, actions may be brought at common law. A good example is the English case of *Whippey v Jones*. The report from the Court of Appeal is recommended reading, not least for the clarity of exposition and application of the basic principles of negligence. The action was brought by a jogger who was knocked by Hector, a Great Dane, as he emerged unexpectedly from behind a bush. Some contact was made and the jogger fell down a bank breaking his ankle. There was no liability under the equivalent English legislation, the Animals Act 1971, but the dog's owner, Mr Whippey was found liable in negligence at first instance. This decision was reversed on appeal. Applying *Donoghue v Stevenson*, *Muir v Glasgow Corporation* and *Bolton v Stone* it was held that there had to be a sufficient probability of injury to lead a reasonable person to anticipate it. In checking that there appeared to be nobody about before releasing the dog from his lead, Whippey had acted as a reasonable dog-owner would, especially in view of the fact that Hector had no known propensity to jump up at people. Mr Whippey's actions had not fallen below the standard of care and so he was not negligent.

Finally, the Animals (Scotland) Act provides in s.4, defences to a civil action brought for killing or injuring an animal. This is a completely separate matter from the general subject matter of the Act and needs to be understood as such. Section 4(1)(a) may be cited in defence where an animal has been killed or injured: (i) in self-defence; (ii) to protect another person; or (iii) to protect livestock. Various conditions must be met for this defence to be upheld. In all cases the police must have been informed within 48 hours of the incident (s.4(1)(b)). The s.4(1)(a)(iii) defence of acting to protect livestock is only available to certain persons specified in s.4(3). These are: the keeper of the livestock; the owner or occupier of the land on which the livestock is present; or a person authorised by either of the former two to act for protection of the livestock. All three defences are further subject to conditions set out in s.4(4). The broad effect of these conditions is that the defender must have acted out of necessity and with little alternative option available. The defence is lost where the killing or injury occurred at or near a place where the defender was present for purposes of engaging in criminal activity and was in furtherance of that activity. If A kills B's dog while it has its jaws clamped around his thigh then, when B sues A for damages, A can defend the action provided he has informed the police within the set time. Where, however, A was burgling B's house at the time the defence is lost.

PRODUCT LIABILITY

Damage caused by a defective product incurs strict liability under the **6–05** Consumer Protection Act 1987. Liability cannot be excluded by contractual term or notice (s.7). The Act does not cover any damage to the defective product itself and the common law continues to operate. Section 1(2) defines a product as any goods or electricity and includes component parts and raw materials. Goods are widely defined in s.45. Case law covers such diverse products as: blood transfusions (*A v National Blood Authority (No.1)*); breast implants (*Hems v Poly Implants Prosthesis*); and motorbikes (*Baker v KTM Motorrad AG*). A product is defective if it is not as safe, generally, as persons are entitled to expect (s.3(1)). It is relevant to consider the marketing and presentation of the product, any instructions or warnings and the use to which the product might be expected to be put (s.3(2)). The Act covers damage in the form of personal injury or death and damage to property intended for private use, occupation or consumption. This reflects the fact that the Act is primarily intended to protect consumers. In *Renfrew Golf Club v Motorcaddy Ltd* pursuers failed to obtain damages against the supplier of an electric golf caddy, a defect in which had caused it to catch fire and damage the clubhouse in which it was kept. The clubhouse was deemed to be commercial premises and not therefore within the scope of the Act. Section 5(4) excludes claims with a value of £275 or less.

The parties liable are listed in s.2(2). These are: the producer; any party holding themselves out as producer, e.g. where a product is sold under the retailer's brand; and any party importing the product into the EU. Suppliers may be liable under s.2(3) if they have failed to respond within a reasonable time to a request to identify any of the three parties listed in s.2(2). Section 2(5) provides that where more than one party is liable, liability is joint and several. Defences are provided in s.4. It is a defence to show: that the defect arose from compliance with a regulation; that the defender never supplied the product; that the defect did not exist at the time of supply (see e.g. *Piper v JRI (Manufacturing) Ltd*); that the defect was undiscoverable due to the state of scientific or technological knowledge at the time of supply; or that defect was attributable to the later addition of a component following the time of supply. Finally, in s.4(1)(c) there is an exemption where products are supplied outwith the course of business. The exemption applies to persons not covered in s.2(2), i.e. they are not the producer or importer or, where they are, the supply is not for profit. This exempts the bakers of cakes and makers of jam for church coffee mornings and suchlike from strict liability under the Act and should perhaps be known as the home-made jam exception.

FRAUD

The institutional definition of fraud is "a machination or contrivance to **6–06** deceive, by words or acts" (Bell, *Principles*, para.13). Fraud is established where an untrue statement or representation is made, or where the statement is believed to be untrue or where the person making the statement is recklessly indifferent to its truth or falsity (*Derry v Peek*). Fraud is an intentional delict leading normally to economic loss. The restrictions on recovery of damages for pure economic loss found in negligence do not apply in intentional delicts.

In civil law, fraud arises most often in the context of misrepresentation in contract. In such circumstances, fraud gives rise to both delictual and contractual remedies. For example, in the case of *Smith v Sim* the pursuer bought a pub in Montrose relying on turnover figures produced by the defender. The figures turned out to be fraudulent. Under the law of contract, Smith had the right to have the contract reduced. The fact that he chose not to exercise this right did not preclude him from recovering damages in delict in respect of fraud. As an alternative to damages, fraud may give rise to a right to restitution or recompense. For example, where a trader has fraudulently persuaded a person to part with a valuable painting, it may be preferable for the victim to secure the return of the painting rather than to be compensated in damages.

PASSING OFF

6–07 Broadly, passing off is an attempt by a trader to appropriate the goodwill of another trader. This occurs where the name or "get up" of a product is sufficiently similar to another product to amount to a misrepresentation that will confuse consumers. Loss is in the form of reduced sales or damaged reputation. The primary remedy in cases of passing off is interdict. Damages may also be available, although the process of quantifying loss may present problems. Courts can of course be asked to calculate quantum in an action for count, reckoning and payment. While the effect of the law is to protect market share, sales and reputation, these are interlinked in the concept of goodwill and so the interest protected is the pursuer's interest in intangible assets. Wrongful appropriation of goodwill in the form of passing off is a delict; other interferences with incorporeal moveable property such as breach of patent and copyright fall to be treated under the law of intellectual property. That is a specialised branch of property law and statutory regimes apply.

The essential elements of passing off are set out by Lord Diplock in *Erven Warnink BV v J Townend & Sons (Hull) Ltd (No.1)*. First, there is a misrepresentation. Second, the misrepresentation is made by a trader in the course of trade. Third, the misrepresentation is made to prospective customers of theirs or ultimate consumers of goods and services provided by them. Fourth, the misrepresentation is calculated to injure the business or goodwill of another trader. Fifth, the misrepresentation has caused or probably will cause damage to the business or goodwill of the other trader.

When Borden started selling lemon juice in lemon shaped containers the House of Lords held that this amounted to a misrepresentation that would confuse shoppers who would think they were buying Jif lemon juice. The manufacturers of Jif had marketed their product in similar containers for some 35 years and had 75 per cent market share in the UK. The injunction awarded by the trial judge was upheld (*Reckitt & Colman Products Ltd v Borden Inc (No.3)*). A well-known Scottish example is provided by the 1954 case, *John Haig and Co Ltd v Forth Blending Co Ltd*. The petitioners had sold a brand of whisky, Dimple, in a highly distinctively shaped bottle since 1910. The respondents started selling their own whisky in an identically shaped bottle, albeit there was little risk of confusion while the bottles remained unopened since the labelling of each was different and the respondents' bottle was stopped with a cork while the Haig bottle used a patent stopper. The scope for confusion arose, however, when stoppers were removed from bottles supplied to pubs and replaced by pourers. Indeed, most of the respondents' whisky was supplied to pubs. The Lord Ordinary (Hill-Watson) considered that the respondents had appropriated so much of the petitioners' "get up" as to enable unscrupulous retailers to sell measures of the respondents' whisky as Dimple. Interdict was granted. A contrary example is provided by *Stringfellow v McCain Foods (GB) Ltd*. In that case it was held that marketing oven chips under the name "stringfellows" was not a misrepresentation. The scope for confusing chips with a famous nightclub is perhaps limited. *Fage UK Ltd v Chobani UK Ltd* demonstrates the concept of extended goodwill. This refers to attributes of a product independent of the maker's brand. The applicant held 95 per cent of the UK market in Greek yoghurt. The respondent started selling product labelled as "Greek yoghurt", although it was made in the USA. Since it appeared highly likely that the petitioner would establish that Greek yoghurt had special characteristics that distinguished it from "Greek-style" yoghurt the respondents agreed to submit to the court their plans for remedial action.

THE ECONOMIC DELICTS

Inducing breach of contract

There are three economic delicts properly so-called. These are inducing breach **6–08** of contract, causing loss by unlawful means and conspiracy. This categorisation follows the model established by the House of Lords in *OBG v Allan*. Liability for inducing breach of contract arises when A induces B to breach her contract with C causing C to suffer economic loss. B will be liable to C for breach of contract and A will be liable to C in delict. The requirements for liability are set out in *Global Resources Group v Mackay*. First, there must have been a breach; A must have known of the contract; A must have intended to induce the breach; A must in fact have induced the breach. Case law suggests that sufficient knowledge may be inferred from a conscious decision not to enquire into the possibility of contractual terms or their breach (see e.g. *Rossleigh Ltd v Leader Cars Ltd*). In *Mainstream Properties Ltd v Young* a financier had purchased development land in conjunction with two employees of the claimant who acted in breach of their contracts of employment. The financier was not liable because he had positively sought assurances from the employees and honestly believed that their joint venture would not breach their contracts.

Causing loss by unlawful means

6–09 This delict arises when A uses unlawful means against B to cause economic loss to C. A will become liable to C in damages. Unlawful means, in this context, is action that would make A civilly liable to B and that limits B's freedom to deal with C. For example, if A breaches a contract to supply materials to B that renders B unable to manufacture product for C, this is unlawful means since A would be liable to B for breach of contract. In *OBG v Allan* the claimant sought damages after receivers had been appointed by an unsecured creditor. The receivers had terminated most of OBG's contracts. It was held by a majority in the House of Lords that there had been no breach or non-performance of any contract, so there could be no liability for inducing breach of contract. Although the claimant had contended that the receivers had been wrongly appointed, it was held that since they acted in good faith and had employed neither unlawful means nor intended loss to the claimants, there was no liability for causing loss by unlawful means. The requirement for liability of subjective intent to harm is confirmed in *Mainstream Properties Ltd v Young*. It may be that the threat of an unlawful act will satisfy the requirements of this delict. In *Rookes v Barnard (No.1)* three trade union officials threatened their employer, BOAC, with an unlawful strike action unless Rookes' employment was terminated. Rookes succeeded in his case against the three officials. This was regarded at the time as a case of intimidation, but it appears from *OBG v Allan* that intimidation is covered under causing loss by unlawful means.

Conspiracy

6–10 While it is not an actionable delict for commercial concerns to attempt to drive their competitors out of business, for example, by undercutting prices (see *Allen v Flood*), where two or more parties combine with the intention of causing economic harm, then delictual liability may arise. So a course of action that would not be wrongful if carried out by a single party becomes actionable by virtue of conspiracy. There are two forms of conspiracy, termed "lawful means" and "unlawful means" respectively. Where two or more parties act in combination, employing lawful means to do so, there will be no liability unless it can be shown that harm to the pursuer was the predominant motive. This follows from the leading case on conspiracy, *Crofter Hand Woven Harris Tweed Co Ltd v Veitch*. In that case the predominant motive of the defenders was to advance the aims of a trades union and loss to the pursuers was incidental. There was therefore no liability. The onus is on the pursuer to establish predominant motive to harm. The pursuer must also establish economic loss. Where the means used are unlawful, in the sense of being criminal, in breach of contract, in breach of statute or a delict, then the pursuer has to establish that the conspirators intended harm, but in such circumstances harm need not be the predominant motive for the conduct.

7. GENERAL MATTERS

VICARIOUS LIABILITY

Vicarious liability operates to make one party liable for the delict of another **7–01** on the basis that it is fair and just that the first party should do so. A wrongfully harms B and B recovers her losses from C. Clearly C is not some randomly selected individual, this would not be just. Vicarious liability depends on a relationship between A and C. Classically this relationship has been one of employment so C can be called to answer to B for A's wrongful conduct where C is A's employer. The other essential factor is the connection between the wrongful act and the relationship linking the parties. It is not sufficient for vicarious liability that wrongdoer and defender are linked by a relationship, the wrongful conduct must be sufficiently connected to that relationship. This point completes our basic model. C will be vicariously liable to B for A's wrongful conduct where C is A's employer and A's delict is sufficiently connected to his employment for it to be fair and just that C should be called upon to answer for it. This adequately describes most instances of vicarious liability in which the issue is not contentious, however it is not a sufficient explanation of the law in more difficult cases. The issues of relationship and conduct need further discussion, but this model will serve to get the ball rolling.

Vicarious liability is a form of strict liability. The employer will not usually be at fault, though it is possible for the employer to be both vicariously and personally liable to the victim. So, for example, if C employs A to make deliveries and, in the process of doing so, A crashes the works van into B's car in breach of the duty A owes to other road users in the vicinity, then C will be vicariously liable to B for A's conduct even though C personally owed no duty to B. Where on the other hand, C employs A to operate a fork lift truck in C's warehouse and, while visiting the warehouse, B is injured by A's negligent use of the fork lift then C may be both vicariously liable to B for C's delict and personally liable to B under occupiers' liability for a danger due to things done on the premises.

Vicarious liability is joint and several. It is competent to pursue both the wrongdoer as personally liable and the employer as vicariously liable. The employer is much more likely to be able to settle the claim; that indeed is the practical point of vicarious liability. Van drivers and fork lift truck operators don't earn vast sums and employers will always be covered by insurance. Vicarious liability gives the victim a party worth suing. Because liability is joint and several, on settling the claim the employer may then proceed to recover the sum paid from the employee (see e.g. *Lister v Romford Ice & Cold Storage Ltd*). As in any case of joint and several liability, contributions to damages may be apportioned by the court. Recovery of sums paid from the employee is, however, only rarely a practical possibility for obvious reasons. While the former is more common, vicarious liability may arise in respect of both negligent and intentional wrongdoing. Case law in which vicarious liability has been imposed for intentional acts includes, for example: *Neville v C & A Modes* (defamation), *Morris v CW Martin and Sons* (theft); *Taylor v Glasgow District Council* (fraud); and *Photo Production Ltd v Securicor* (wilful fire raising). Child sex abuse has given rise to vicarious liability in a number of cases.

Various justifications for vicarious liability have been advanced. The concept of agency was central in the early development of the doctrine with the maxim *qui facit per alium facit* per se (roughly, someone who acts through another acts themselves) employed as an explanation. This approach proved less satisfactory as vicarious liability expanded to include acts that the employer had not authorised and eventually came to cover acts expressly forbidden. A more satisfactory rationale in the modern context is that the party whose enterprise is being advanced ought in fairness to bear the risks entailed in the pursuit of the enterprise. To return to an example used earlier, if C employs A to drive a van there is a risk that A will drive negligently and cause harm so C must bear the consequences of that risk if it materialises. It is a risk arising from the conduct of C's business. It may be noted that where vicarious liability arises, any defences available to the wrongdoer are also available to the employer. The employer cannot, however, evade liability on the basis of care taken in selecting the employee or on the basis that the employee acted contrary to instruction. In *Rose v Plenty* a milkman hired a 13-year-old boy to assist with deliveries in flagrant breach of dairy policy. The boy was injured when the milkman drove the float negligently. The dairy was found vicariously liable since the boy's presence on the float was in pursuit of the employer's business.

Relationships and conduct

7–02 Vicarious liability was never entirely restricted to relationships of employment. In origin, it applied between master and servant, but it has long been settled that vicarious liability can arise between principal and agent and between partners in partnership. Otherwise, it was established during the 19th century that a relationship of employment was a necessary condition with the critical distinction drawn between employees, for whom the employer was liable, and independent contractors for whose delicts the party instructing could not be held liable. A relationship of employment could, of course, be established where a contract of employment was in place, but circumstances are not always so straightforward and the issue generated a lot of case law. For a long time the control test was applied to determine whether relationships amounted to employment. Under this test one party was the employer if they could tell the other not only what to do, but how to do it. This approach had severe limitations when applied to skilled workers. Rather than apply a single test, courts developed a more flexible approach taking a number of factors into account according to the circumstances. Examples of this flexibility can be seen in *Short v J&W Henderson Ltd* and *United Wholesale Grocers Ltd v Sher.* Changing work arrangements, casualisation of the workforce in general, zero hours contracts, an increasing use of agency workers and, indeed, unpaid internships have brought into question the appropriateness of the employment/independent contractor dichotomy as a basis upon which to determine vicarious liability. The underlying policy concern is that, while the law cannot guarantee compensation to victims in every circumstance, innocent third parties should not be denied an effective remedy simply because of contractual arrangements or lack of them between the wrongdoer and the party for whom they were acting.

The law has indeed moved on, but before the present law is considered some coverage of the issue of conduct may be useful for two reasons. One reason is that, as in the relationship issue, past tests to determine whether conduct is covered by vicarious liability or not have proved problematic. The other is that the new approach ties the issues of relationship and conduct together so they are no longer entirely discrete questions.

The fact that A is employed by C does not make C answerable for all A's delicts. Until 2001 when the House of Lords adopted the "sufficient connection" test in *Lister v Hesley Hall*, conduct falling within the scope of the wrongdoer's employment incurred vicarious liability, conduct outside the scope of employment did not. Both authorised and unauthorised modes of carrying out the task instructed fell within the scope of employment, but employers could not be held vicariously liable for delicts committed when the employee was "off on a frolic of his own". The test derives from *Kirby v NCB* in which employers were not liable to a miner injured by an explosion in the pit caused when a match was lit. Those responsible had gone for a smoke to a part of the pit away from where they had been working. Similar to the relationship issue, determining whether conduct was within the scope of employment was not always straightforward and, again, courts demonstrated some flexibility. This may be seen in the "deviation" cases. When a lorry driver collided with a car, his employers argued unsuccessfully that the driver was acting outwith the scope of his employment since he was off-route having gone a couple of miles out of his way to collect his spectacles (*Angus v Glasgow Corporation*). An employee who had been allowed to take a van home crashed it, damaging a bridge. Contrary to instruction, the driver had gone out of his way, first to drop off a mate and then to visit his mother-in-law. This did not prevent vicarious liability. The Lord Ordinary (Wylie) held that the original, authorised purpose of the journey had not been wholly superseded and so the conduct fell within the scope of employment (*RJ McLeod v South of Scotland Electricity Board*). These cases follow a decision of the House of Lords from 1966, *Williams v Hemphill*. A driver employed to take a company of the boys' brigade from camp in Knapdale home to Glasgow, acceded to a request from the boys to travel via Dollar so that they could meet up with a party of girl guides. The driver overturned the lorry near Dollar and his employer was liable to those injured or killed. The dominant purpose of the journey was transportation of the boys to Glasgow, the driver was still engaged in this purpose and the deviation by Dollar was not an independent journey. The flaw in the scope of employment approach became apparent in *Trotman v North Yorkshire County Council*. A schoolteacher was tasked with taking a disabled teenage boy on a foreign holiday and took the opportunity to sexually abuse his charge. The Court of Appeal determined that the employer was not vicariously liable. Far from being an unauthorised mode of carrying out a duty, the acts were held to be a negation of the duty and thus independent of employment.

Recent developments

7–03 While changing employment conditions suggested some need for revision, the real prompt to changes in the law has been intentional wrongdoing, particularly in the form of child sexual abuse. *Trotman* was over-ruled in *Lister v Hesley Hall* in which the managers of a boarding school were held vicariously liable for acts of abuse carried out on residents by a warden. A new approach was instituted based on a sufficient connection between the delict and employment. Further developments have been prompted by sexual abuse carried out by members of religious bodies who were not employees. In *E v English Province of Our Lady of Charity* a priest had been abusing children in a children's home. Priests are not employed, but they are answerable to their diocesan bishop and the defendant trust was sued as representing the bishop. McDuff J at first instance challenged the dependence of vicarious liability on employment in the circumstances when the priest had clearly been authorised by the trust to act on its behalf. This approach was upheld in the Court of Appeal and affirmed by the Supreme Court in *Various Claimants v Catholic Child Welfare Society* (the *Christian Brothers* case). In that case children in a residential home had been sexually abused by monks. It is now the case that vicarious liability arises from relationships of employment and relationships "akin to employment". The point is summarised by Lord Reed in the Supreme Court in the later case of *Cox v Ministry of Justice*.

> "A relationship other than employment is in principle capable of giving rise to vicarious liability where harm is wrongfully done by an individual who carries on activities as an integral part of the business activities carried on by a defendant and for its benefit (rather than his activities being entirely attributable to the conduct of a recognisably independent business of his own or of a third party), and where the commission of the wrongful act is a risk created by the defendant by assigning those activities to the individual in question."

Cox concerned the negligence of a prisoner who injured the prison catering manager when he dropped a sack of flour. The prison authorities were held vicariously liable. Prisoners are not employees, but this prisoner had been assigned to kitchen duties integral to the running of the prison and undertaken in furtherance of its aims. It will be noted that Lord Reed does not confine the coverage of his remarks to the relationship element, but includes reference to the conduct in question. The prisoner had been placed by the authorities in a position where there was a risk that he would be negligent within the field of activities assigned to him. In this way both relationship and conduct are linked in the process of determining vicarious liability. Another Supreme Court case of the same time, *Mohamud v Wm Morrison Supermarkets Plc*, dealt with the question of conduct and the judgments in the two cases are complementary to one another. Khan, an employee in a petrol station racially abused and seriously assaulted Mohamud who had called in to enquire whether he could print documents from a USB stick. Khan's response was "we don't do such shit". He then ordered Mohamud off the premises and followed him to his car before assaulting him. The question arose whether Khan's employers should be vicariously liable. The approach set out by Lord Toulson was a development on the sufficient connection test established in *Lister*. First, a broad view of the functions or field of activities assigned to the wrongdoer should be taken once the nature of the wrongdoer's job is ascertained. Second, the court must determine whether the conduct was sufficiently connected to the position in which the wrongdoer was employed for it to be just to hold the employer vicariously liable. On a broad view, Khan's job was to attend to customers and answer their enquiries. Since, in seeing Mohamud off the premises, Khan was purporting to go about his employers' business, the second determination was answered in the affirmative. Lord Toulson observed:

> "It was a gross abuse of his position, but it was in connection with the business in which he was employed to serve customers. His employers entrusted him with that position and it is just that as between them and the claimant, they should be held responsible for their employee's abuse of it."

The connection to be sought then is between the wrongful act and the relationship. Has the position in which the employer has placed the wrongdoer created the risk of the act? Whether the employer was careless in appointing the wrongdoer to the job is irrelevant. Vicarious liability does not require fault on the employer's part and any employee can be negligent or badly behaved. Khan was employed to attend to customers and he did so, albeit in a highly unpleasant fashion. It may be notable that Khan was deemed to have abused his position and also that the victim was a third party entitled to regard Khan as a representative of his employers. When employees injure their fellow employees, employers will not be liable simply because the incident occurred in the workplace. Had Khan stolen from a colleague's handbag, for example, a finding of vicarious liability would have been unlikely because the necessary connection between his role in attending to customers and his conduct would have been absent. Much of the case law pre-dating *Mohamud* remains relevant. In *Ward v Scotrail* employers were not vicariously liable when a ticket collector suffered the unwanted attentions of a fellow employee. Employment provided the opportunity, but the conduct was a purely personal matter.

Similar results are found in: *Wilson v Excel Ltd* in which the pursuer had had her ponytail pulled by a supervisor; *Vaikuviene v J Sainsbury Plc*, which involved a racially motivated murder; and *Sommerville v Harsco* in which a supervisor threw a hammer at a scaffold worker with whom he was having a bit of banter. The hammer hit the pursuer, another scaffold worker, instead.

The present position

7–04 The question whether vicarious liability arises resolves into a two-part test: whether the relevant relationship was one of employment or akin to employment; and, if so, whether the wrongful act was sufficiently closely connected with that employment or quasi-employment for it to be fair and just to call upon the defender to answer for it.

Although vicarious liability does not, in the words of Lord Reed, extend to activities "entirely attributable to the conduct of a recognisably independent business of his [the wrongdoer's] own or of a third party", it is apparent that the critical distinction is between parties for whom the defender is vicariously liable and parties for whom he is not, rather than between employers and independent contractors. The consequences of this change have yet to be fully worked out. Five factors relevant to addressing the question were set out by Lord Phillips in the *Christian Brothers* case. These were later discussed by Lord Reed in *Cox*. Lord Reed expressed the view that the more important factors pointing in the direction of vicarious liability are: commission of the wrong as a result of activity carried out on behalf of the defender; the wrongdoer's conduct or activity being part of the defender's business activities; and the business activity having created the risk of the wrongdoing. Business is to be viewed broadly and is by no means restricted to commercial activities or those carried out for profit. Lord Reed thought less weight should be attached to the remaining two factors: the fact that defenders are more likely to be insured did not provide a principled basis for vicarious liability and the final factor, the defender's control over the wrongdoer, was in his view "unlikely to be of independent significance in most cases". Expect to see further discussion on these factors. In *Armes v Nottinghamshire County Council* Lord Hughes (dissenting) considered that the only helpful factors were the degree of integration of the wrongdoer into the defender's business activities and the element of control.

In *Armes* a majority in the Supreme Court held a local authority vicariously liable to claimants who had been physically and sexually abused as children in foster care. Foster parents, it was held, provide care to children as an integral part of the authorities' organisation of its child care services. Subsequently, the Court of Appeal has upheld a decision to hold a bank vicariously liable in respect of 126 complaints brought by women who had been subjected to unnecessary intimate examinations by a general medical practitioner conducting medicals on new employees for the bank (*Various Claimants v Barclays Bank Plc*). The following text is representative of the current approach, it refers to the judge's findings at first instance and it is extracted directly from the case report:

"She found that the tort was committed as a result of activity undertaken by the doctor on behalf of the bank; was for the bank's benefit and an integral part of its business activity; that the doctor was working under the bank's control in respect of the nature of the medical assessments and completion of the reports; and that the bank was more likely to have the means to compensate the victims and could be expected to be insured against such liability. She concluded that the tort was sufficiently closely connected with the bank's quasi-employment of the doctor, and that it was fair and just to find the bank vicariously liable."

Temporary employees and dual vicarious liability

Where an employee is lent by one concern to another, the question of which **7–05** employer should be vicariously liable for wrongs committed while on loan has traditionally been addressed by the doctrine of *pro hac vice* employment. The employer who borrows the person will only become vicariously liable if it can be established that full control over not only what the employee does, but how the employee does it, has passed to the borrowing employer. *Pro hac vice* employment is not determined by any contractual agreement between the two employers. Thus, even though a contract provides that the party is to be regarded as a servant of the borrowing employer, this cannot be relied upon in an issue with a third party who was not a party to the contract. In the House of Lords case of *Mersey Docks and Harbour Board v Coggins & Griffith (Liverpool) Ltd* the defendants, a firm of stevedores, borrowed a crane and driver from the Harbour Board. It was held that, while the firm told the crane driver what to do, the way in which he did it was a matter within his own discretion. This discretion had been delegated to him by the Harbour Board. When the crane driver negligently injured an employee of Coggins & Griffith, the Harbour Board was held vicariously liable.

While *pro hac vice* employment remains law, where an employee is sufficiently integrated into both businesses, a more recent development has been a willingness of the courts to hold both vicariously liable. This development stems from *Viasystems (Tyneside) Ltd v Thermal Transfer (Northern) Ltd*, approved by the Supreme Court in the *Christian Brothers* case. To reach a finding of dual vicarious liability, the relationship between the wrongdoer and each defender must be considered independently. The test is not one of control, but concerns the extent to which the wrongdoer was integrated into the work, business or organisation of the defenders and whether this was sufficient to make it fair and just to impose vicarious liability on them both. *Mersey Docks* was distinguished in *Christian Brothers* and so *pro hac vice* employment remains based on control.

NON-DELEGABLE DUTIES

Non-delegable duties concern personal and not vicarious liability. When a **7–06** duty is non-delegable this means that the party owing the duty will be liable even though the harm was incurred through the conduct of a third party. Effectively, the consequences of breach fall on the party that owed the duty even though that duty was breached by another. The rationale behind non-delegable duties is that they can provide compensation to innocent victims in circumstances where vicarious liability does not operate, particularly in cases where the contractor has gone into liquidation. Moreover, when a duty is non-delegable, a party cannot hide behind rules on vicarious liability to evade liability when they have allocated their functions to some hapless contractor. Since the rules on vicarious liability have become more fluid it remains to be seen whether non-delegable duties have much future. It is established that the duty owed by employers to employees to provide a safe system of work is non-delegable (*Wilsons & Clyde Coal Co v English*; *McDermid v Nash Dredging & Reclamation Co Ltd*). Hospitals owe a non-delegable duty to patients in their care in addition to the vicarious liability they may incur through the negligence of staff (see e.g. *Bell v Alliance Medical Ltd*).

Non-delegable duties arise in two contexts. The first involves vulnerability on the part of the victim. The second concerns hazardous activities. In *Woodland v Essex County Council* the Supreme Court imposed liability on an education authority when a child found hanging in the water during a swimming lesson suffered hypoxic brain injury. The child was at the time in the care of a contractor who provided swimming lessons as an integral part of the school curriculum. While the school had delegated the performance functions for which it had assumed responsibility to the contractor, it could not delegate its duty to the child and so was held liable. Lord Sumption considered the authorities and set out to provide a principled basis for the recognition of non-delegable duties of care. First pursuer and defender must be in a relationship that imposes positive duties on the defender to provide care for the defender. This allows for an inference of assumption of responsibility. Second, performance of the duty may be delegated, but the defender remains responsible for ensuring that care functions are performed to the requisite standard and must answer to the pursuer when they are not. Third, where the injury occurs during the performance of functions different from those for which the defender has assumed responsibility, then no non-delegable duty arises, the rules of vicarious liability apply and the defender will evade liability unless it is established that they were negligent in their appointment of the contractor. If, for example, an education authority contracts with a bus company to transport children to and from school, no non-delegable duty would be recognised as owing to children injured by the negligent driving of the bus, because this is not a function that the school would have performed in any case.

The other branch of non-delegable duty is less clear and generally more contentious. This is the rule that a non-delegable duty arises where a party instructs works that are inherently hazardous. The idea is that a party instructing an inherently hazardous (sometimes termed ultra-hazardous) operation should bear the risk for the consequences if damage is caused.

Lord Sumption considered that the authorities on hazardous activities were "ripe for review". It has been argued that this is a rule of English law that has only appeared in Scots law through a mis-reading of the authorities. Nevertheless, there has been some recognition of the point in the Scottish courts, albeit with no real progress on developing anything resembling a coherent doctrine. Some support for the rule is found in the Inner House case *Stewart v Malik*. The pursuer's argument, that a party instructing the removal of a load-bearing wall owed a non-delegable duty to the upper proprietor was accepted. This does have elements in common with the first branch of the rule in that an upper proprietor is especially vulnerable to building operations carried out on the lower property. Also, the lower proprietor did owe a positive duty of support. The need for an antecedent positive duty, however, seems to have been abandoned in the later Outer House case of *Esso Petroleum v Scottish Ministers*. This case involved construction of the M74 extension on contaminated land used previously for the distribution and storage of chemicals. The operation had resulted in the escape of toxic chemicals through subterranean water onto premises owned by the pursuers. The arguments in the case are complicated and involve elements of negligence, nuisance, non-delegable duty and vicarious liability. The Lord Ordinary (Tyrie) held that the Scottish Ministers were not relieved of potential liability by having engaged a competent contractor. Had the Scottish Ministers held their nerve, it would have been interesting to see whether a clearer view of the law would have emerged from an appeal that might reasonably have been anticipated from a decision either way, but the case was settled before proof. The Scots law on non-delegable duties in the context of hazardous operations remains obscure for the time being.

GENERALLY APPLICABLE DEFENCES

Contributory negligence

In an action for damages it is usually open to the defender to plead that the pursuer contributed to some extent to the injury or damage complained of through their own fault. Indeed, in personal injury cases a defence of contributory negligence is more or less routine. At common law, where the pursuer's own contribution to the event was established the defender was exonerated from liability entirely. Unsurprisingly, this led to some unjust decisions, *Grant v Caledonian Railway Co* being a good example. Since the coming into force of the Law Reform (Contributory Negligence) Act 1945, contribution is no longer a complete defence. Where the defence is established, damages will be reduced by a proportion to reflect the pursuer's own contribution. The process can be viewed in terms of two concepts: causative potency and blameworthiness. The former is concerned with causation, specifically the extent to which each party's own actions caused the harm; the second is of a more equitable nature and questions the extent to which each party ought in fairness to be regarded as responsible. A

7–07

common example of contribution is where a passenger in a car is injured as a result of the driver's negligent driving, but injuries are exacerbated because the passenger has failed to wear a seatbelt.

Where contribution is established, courts apportion blame for the damage between the parties and seek to effect a reduction in damages that is just and equitable. For example, in *Sayers v Harlow UDC* damages were reduced by 25 per cent to reflect the plaintiff's own contribution to her injuries. She had been trapped in a public toilet cubicle, but in attempting to climb out was held to have contributed to her losses. Her foot slipped on the toilet roll holder and she fell to the floor. In reducing damages courts must determine the total damages that would have been awarded had there been no contribution by the defender. Thus, we can see the exact apportionment determined by the court. In *Campbell v Gillespie* a mechanic was working at night on a broken down lorry on the A87, between Shiel Bridge and Kyle of Lochalsh. This road may be driven at speed in places and it is not lit. The lorry's lights had been disconnected and the mechanic should have provided protection by parking his own, lit vehicle behind the lorry. There was a police warning sign and other vehicles had avoided the lorry before the pursuer's husband ploughed into the back of it at 60mph, or faster, in his Vauxhall Astra. The car driver was held 60 per cent to blame, the mechanic, 40 per cent.

Occasionally, decisions on apportionment lead to further dispute. In *Jackson v Murray* a 13-year-old girl suffered severe injury crossing the road behind the school bus from which she had alighted. At first instance apportionment was determined at 90 per cent for the girl and 10 per cent for the driver of the car that had run her over. The ratio was changed to 70:30 on reclaiming to the Inner House. Taking into account the finding of the Lord Ordinary, that the defender was driving without reasonable care, he had made no allowance for the potential hazard presented by the school bus and had not slowed down at all, apportionment was set finally at 50:50 in the Supreme Court. It has been suggested that the decision reflects the relative blameworthiness of the parties, the lower courts having perhaps focussed too closely on the causation aspect. It must be noted that appellate courts will not readily interfere with apportionment decisions determined in lower courts except where, as Lord Hodge explained in *Jackson*, the court had "manifestly and to a substantial degree gone wrong".

Volenti non fit injuria

7–08 A further defence is afforded by the doctrine of volenti non fit injuria (to one consenting no wrong is done). Volenti operates where it can be held that the pursuer has consented to the risk undertaken by the defender. Volenti is a complete defence. Where established, it relieves the defender from all liability. It is accordingly a harder defence to establish than contribution. The defender must establish that the pursuer had knowledge of the risk and willingly assented to it. Volenti does not apply to passengers in road vehicles (Road Traffic Act 1988 s.149). No such restriction applies to aircraft. In *Morris v Murray* two friends took off in a light aircraft following an afternoon's heavy drinking. The plane crashed shortly after take-off and the injured passenger sued the pilot's estate. The defence of volenti was successfully established. The passenger knew perfectly well that the pilot had been drinking and, in accepting the lift, was held to have impliedly consented to run the risk of flying with a drunk pilot. It should be noted that volenti is not restricted in scope to negligence actions, but is a generally available defence in delict that can also be found in statutory form, for example in the Occupiers' Liability (Scotland) Act s.2(3). In the assault case of *Reid v Mitchell* it was argued that the pursuer was *volens* of the risk of falling off the haycart. The defence did not succeed since it was found that the pursuer was not a willing participant in the general larking about.

Ex turpi causa non oritur actio
Literally, this means that no action arises from an immoral cause. **7–09** Effectively, it means that no liability arises between parties jointly engaged in a criminal undertaking. So, for example, if two men are engaged in safe blowing in the course of a bank robbery, the negligent accomplice who fires the explosive charge at the wrong time and kills his mate will use this defence if the widow brings an action against him. The defence cannot, however, be used to excuse an assault carried out on a person committing a criminal act (*McLaughlin v Morrison*). Where established, ex turpi causa is a complete defence. It is important to remember, however, that issues of morality, wickedness and, indeed, policy are bound up in this defence—it is not purely concerned with criminal infringements of the law and so it will not apply, for example, against a pursuer whose only criminal act was to park a vehicle on double yellow lines. The case of *Weir v Wyper* demonstrates that courts will not allow this defence without regard to the circumstances. A 16-year-old girl allowed herself to be driven home by a young man who held only a provisional driving license. As such she was jointly engaged in an illegal undertaking and the driver sought to rely upon this when she sued him for damages, an accident having occurred on the way home. In the circumstances, the pursuer had little option but to act as she did. The journey at the outset had been legal since there had been two other passengers, one of whom held a full driving license. This couple, however, had got out of the car in some remote spot, leaving the pursuer a long way from home with a man she barely knew. The defence was not upheld. The English case of *Pitts v Hunt* provides an example in which the defence succeeded. Two young men who had been drinking were involved in an accident in which the rider was killed. The pillion's action against the rider's estate failed. The pillion knew that the rider was unlicensed and uninsured and, moreover, had actively encouraged dangerous and reckless riding to frighten other road users. This defence is not very often used and it raises some difficult issues. Judicial discussion may be found in the House of Lords case *Gray v Thames Trains Ltd*.

Damnum fatale

7–10 In exceptional circumstances a defender may plead *damnum fatale*. Broadly, this means "act of God", equivalent to the defence in English law of *vis major*. In *Kerr v Earl of Orkney* the defender sought to attribute the collapse of his dam to a *damnum fatale*. The court, however, refused to accept that heavy rainfall in Renfrewshire constituted a *damnum fatale* and it was thought much more likely that the dam had failed from insufficiency of construction since it had survived only four months. To succeed as a defence a *damnum fatale* has to be some unpredictable and overpowering event beyond human control, such as a tsunami or volcanic eruption.

Prescription and limitation

7–11 Prescription is a process of time by which rights may be acquired or lost. Obligations prescribe after five years under the Prescription and Limitation (Scotland) Act 1973 s.6. When an obligation prescribes it is extinguished. Limitation does not extinguish an obligation, but acts as a time-bar to prevent actions from being raised. Actions for personal injury, defamation, harassment and under Pt 1 of the Consumer Protection Act 1987 are all subject to three year limitation periods. The clock starts ticking when the right to the action crystallises, that is when there is a concurrence of *damnum* and *injuria*. Generally, that will be when the injury is incurred or becomes apparent, but, in the nature of things, determining that point can become a matter of difficulty. See s.17(2) for the rules in a personal injury cases not involving death and s.18 where death has occurred. The three year, or triennium, limitation rule has given rise to particular difficulties in the context of child sex abuse where the issue is often not raised for many years after the abuse has culminated. The Limitation (Childhood Abuse) (Scotland) Act 2017 removed the limitation period for physical or sexual abuse of children, inserting s.17A into the 1973 Act. Further changes may be anticipated in the event that the Prescription (Scotland) Bill 2018 is enacted.

REMEDIES

7–12 There is a very basic point to be made at the outset. Every action is brought in the process of seeking a specific remedy or a number of different remedies. In general terms of pleadings, the remedies sought are listed under "Conclusions" and so lawyers speak of concluding for damages or interdict or whichever remedy or remedies are requested. Some remedies are available without recourse to law and, of course, solutions acceptable to both disputing parties may be negotiated between themselves or by their respective solicitors. The simplest remedy is self-help. Its most clear application is in trespass. A landowner may construct a fence or dyke to keep other people or animals from straying onto their property. Trespassers may be asked to leave, but the use of force to eject persons from premises or land is contentious. Trees or shrubs that overhang neighbouring property are encroachments and may be lopped or pruned with no right of recourse accruing to the owner. The effects of nuisance may be obviated in appropriate circumstances by simple acts such as keeping windows closed.

Declarator

A person who has been wronged may seek declarator. A declarator is simply **7–13** a statement concerning the rights of the petitioner. For example, a declarator may provide that a state of affairs amounts to a nuisance. Normally an action for declarator will be accompanied by a conclusion for damages or interdict since the award of declarator itself does not compel the defender to do anything, to refrain from doing anything or to pay anything. A declarator may, however, be useful to prevent the running of prescription and in nuisance it will defeat a later defence of acquiescence.

Damages

The purpose of damages is to repair the loss suffered by the pursuer. In **7–14** awarding damages, the courts seek, insofar as is possible, to effect restitutio in integrum, that is to restore pursuers to the position they would have been in had the delict not occurred. There are two forms of damages reflecting two different types of loss: damages come either in the form of *solatium* or they are patrimonial. Patrimonial loss covers all tangible economic losses, including property damage and financial harm. The expression "patrimonial" derives from *patrimonium*, meaning a person's estate. *Solatium* is awarded for forms of loss or injury that may be described as intangible, such as pain and suffering, distress, anxiety, affront and inconvenience. *Solatium* can be understood as covering non-patrimonial forms of loss. It should be borne in mind that the availability of damages for different forms of loss may depend on the basis on which the claim is brought. Patrimonial losses, when proved, are generally recoverable irrespective of the ground or basis for the action. *Solatium* for distress or anxiety will normally be available in cases of intentional harm, for example harassment or defamation, but is not likely to be awarded in cases of negligence where this is the only form of loss alleged or proved. On the other hand, *solatium* will be awarded either on its own or alongside a patrimonial award where personal injury or property damage have been caused negligently. There is then some relationship between the wrong done and the losses recoverable that is best explored with reference to the particular wrong and the particular loss or injury in each case. It is thought that Scots courts do not make awards of aggravated damages as a separate head, but where a wrong has been aggravated, where for example the defender has protracted litigation by insisting on a defence that they have been unable to establish (see e.g. *Baigent v BBC*), the sum awarded in *solatium* may be enlarged to reflect the aggravation. Claims for damages normally also include a claim for interest on the sum claimed dated back to the time of the event. Some benefits that the pursuer may have received are deducted from awards. Principally, this means that social security payments are repaid to the Department of Work and Pensions, but certain other benefits, such as a benevolent payment made directly by the defender will also reduce damages. Where an award is made for loss of earnings, income tax, national insurance contributions and pension contributions must all be deducted.

Damages at common law

7–15 Where the harm sustained is property damage the process of assessing the quantum (amount) of damages is relatively straightforward. The pursuer may recover from the defender the cost of repairing or replacing the property or a sum to represent any diminution in its value. Claims are calculated at market value. Reasonable expenses are also recoverable, so if a car is damaged through negligence the defender may be held liable to pay the costs of a hire car while the original vehicle is being fixed. *Solatium* claims generally fall under the common law. In personal injury cases *solatium* for pain and suffering is dependent on the awareness of the pursuer and so is not available in respect of any period spent, for example in a coma. *Solatium* in respect of any physical or mental impairment is not similarly dependent. The pursuer may also have a patrimonial claim for past losses, that is loss of net earnings between the incident and date of proof and outlays, such as reasonable medical expenses, are recoverable at common law. Where the earning ability of the pursuer has been affected, the biggest part of the claim is normally for loss of future earnings, which also falls under the common law. Net earnings and any costs of caring for the victim are taken as the multiplicand and multiplied by a factor determined by the pursuer's age and other relevant considerations. This produces a lump sum that, when invested, should provide an annual income equivalent to the loss. The multiplier is selected by use of actuarial tables and the assumed rate of return is updated when necessary by statutory instrument to reflect changes in economic circumstances. Further developments may be anticipated on the enactment of the Damages (Investment Returns and Periodical Payments) (Scotland) Bill 2018, before Parliament at the time of writing.

Statutory claims in respect of personal injury and death

7–16 In cases where the life expectancy of the pursuer has been shortened, the Damages (Scotland) Act 2011 s.1 provides both a *solatium* and a patrimonial claim. The pursuer must be aware of shortened life expectancy for *solatium*, but may recover patrimonial losses irrespective of awareness. The patrimonial claim is calculated by first quantifying the "lost period", which is the time by which the pursuer's life expectancy has been shortened as a result of the delict s.1(5). The sum of earnings and benefits that would have been expected during this period is calculated and then subjected to reduction by 25 per cent. The 25 per cent reduction represents ordinary living expenses. That is money that the pursuer will no longer have to spend and so it is not a loss. The court has powers under s.1(7) to vary the percentage to avoid over or under-compensation. A person on a very high income is unlikely to spend as much as 25 per cent of it on living expenses, whereas someone on a very low income is likely to spend a much greater proportion in order to get by.

Section 8 of the Administration of Justice Act 1982 provides for a patrimonial claim to reimburse relatives for necessary services rendered to the victim in consequence of injuries received by paying them reasonable remuneration and reasonable expenses. Section 9 of the same Act provides for a claim in compensation of personal services that, as a result of injury, the victim is no longer able to render to relatives. The services covered in this claim are those that the victim might be expected to perform for a relative without payment, but for which another person would charge (s.9(3)). In short, where victims are no longer able to coach their children at football or tennis or tutor them on the piano or keep their mother's garden tidy, the expense of employing another person to do the job is recoverable. Note that both the s.8 and s.9 claims can cover future as well as past losses. Note also that only the victim can raise these claims, an obligation falls on the pursuer to reimburse relatives with sums awarded in s.8 claims (s.8(2)). The lack of an equivalent provision in s.9 indicates that pursuers may pay any new service provider directly.

Where the victim dies, s.2 of the 2011 Act allows for all claims incurred to the date of death to transmit to the victim's executor, who may then pursue any action on behalf of the deceased's estate. The exception is damages in respect of injury to name or reputation, effectively defamation, in which case the claim transmits only where an action has been raised and is not concluded by the time of death (s.2(3)). Claims for future losses do not transmit to the executor. The claim for these losses will now constitute part of the relatives' claim.

The relatives' claim

Relatives only have a claim in their own right where the victim dies. Their **7–17** claim rests on the basis that the defender was liable to the victim or would have been so had the victim lived (2011 Act s.3). Relatives have both a patrimonial claim for loss of support and a claim for *solatium* known as "loss of society". The loss of society claim is available to immediate family only, that is the spouse or civil partner, children, grandchildren, parents and grandparents of the deceased. The loss of support claim is available to immediate family and any other relative actually supported by the deceased. The definition of a relative is found in s.14(1).

Section 4(3)(a) provides for the claim for loss of support calculated from the date of death and also for the recovery of reasonable expenses, such as funeral costs. The loss of support element is calculated according to rules in s.7 and is based on 75 per cent of the victim's net income (on the notion that 25 cent represents the personal living costs of the victim) multiplied by a factor determined by the court. The court has power to vary the percentage to avoid "a manifestly and materially unfair result" (s.7(2)). Relatives other than spouses (or civil partners or cohabitants) and dependent children will be compensated only to the extent that they were actually supported by the deceased, the residue going to the spouse and dependent children. If no other relative was supported then the entire award goes to the spouse and dependent children. When the victim dies, the claim for future loss of personal services rendered to relatives by the victim now falls under s.6 of the 2011 Act and is part of the relatives' claim. The services covered remain as set out in s.9(3) of the 1982 Act.

The *solatium* claim for loss of society falls under s.4(3)(b) and represents sums to compensate: (i) distress and anxiety endured in contemplation of the victim's suffering; (ii) grief and sorrow caused by death; and (iii) the loss of non-patrimonial benefits that would have come from the victim had he or she lived, in other words the absence of the deceased is recognised as a loss that goes beyond the purely financial and which should be compensated.

It can be seen that the policy behind the law is that compensation should be directed where the loss is felt, so injured victims will receive damages both for suffering and any inability to support themselves and their families. Where victims are killed outright they have no claim, the relatives experience the entire loss and so they will be compensated in the victim's stead. Where the victim is injured and then dies later, provided the action for damages has not been excluded or settled before death (s.4(2)), compensation is split between the victim and the relatives. In such a case the largest part of the claim, the patrimonial claim for future loss of earnings will go to the latter in the form of loss of support, leaving the victim's own award to go into his or her estate to be distributed according to the law of succession.

Provisional damages

7–18 Where it is proved or admitted that there is a risk that the pursuer's health or condition will seriously deteriorate in the future, s.12 of the Administration of Justice Act 1982 provides that a provisional award of damages may be made. Such an award is only permissible where the defender is a public authority or is insured. A provisional award of damages means that the pursuer may seek further damages in future if the risk of serious deterioration materialises. At that stage it will be possible to assess the extent of pain and suffering or any reasonable expenses. It is within the discretion of the court to set a time limit against future claims. Following the decision of the House of Lords in *Rothwell v Chemical and Insulation Co Ltd* the Scottish Parliament has enacted the Damages (Asbestos-Related Conditions) (Scotland) Act 2009. In *Rothwell* pleural plaques were held not to be material harm though they are an indicator that there has been exposure to asbestos and so there is a possibility of asbestos related illness arising in the future. The Scottish courts have made awards of provisional damages in the past where pleural plaques have been identified and this legislation is intended to allow this to continue.

Interim damages

7–19 The court may grant an award of interim damages before the process of litigation is concluded. Interim payments will only be awarded where liability is admitted by the defender or where there appears no question that the pursuer will succeed. This also means that there should no prospect of a substantial reduction of damages on grounds of contributory negligence.

Interdict

The essence of interdict is that prevention is better than cure. Interdict is **7–20** sought to prevent an anticipated wrong or to put an end to a continuing wrong. An interdict restrains the activities of the party against whom it is awarded. In short, it forbids the party interdicted from conducting the activity specified, at least, not in such a way as to give rise to a legal wrong. The terms of the interdict must be no wider than necessary to curb the wrong complained of. If the terms of the interdict are breached, the party in breach will be liable to a fine or imprisonment. The party seeking the interdict is the petitioner. The party against whom the interdict is sought is the respondent.

Interdict has no real application in negligence. Interdict is an appropriate remedy in delicts of intention, for example, in defamation, trespass, nuisance or harassment. Interdict may be used to protect intellectual property rights and is generally applicable in the economic delicts. Interdicts must be framed in clear and precise terms so that the party interdicted should be left in no doubt regarding the forbidden activity.

Interdicts may be permanent—that is, made without limit of time—or interim. An interim interdict is an immediate remedy that may be applied for at any stage in the process of application for a permanent interdict. For example, if an interdict is sought to prevent publication of defamatory material in a newspaper, an interim interdict may be required if intended publication is imminent. The award of a permanent interdict requires more time and justification, and will not help the petitioner if the material is published before the court reaches a conclusion. The interim interdict serves the purpose of preventing publication, while the more detailed consideration required for permanent interdict takes place.

Interim interdicts are awarded at the court's discretion. There must be a prima facie case; in other words, on the basis of the petitioner's pleadings, it must appear that a relevant case in defamation, or nuisance or whatever wrong is complained of, has been made out. The court will then consider the balance of convenience between the parties. For example, it may be argued that the award of interdict will cause a greater wrong to the respondent than the wrong complained of by the petitioner. Any public interest in the activity complained of will be taken into account by the court. Only where the balance of convenience is held to be in the petitioner's favour will interim interdict be granted. An interim interdict is valid until recalled by the court.

In general interdict is only awarded where there is a genuine prospect of future wrongs. Interdict is not competent in respect of an activity that is unlikely to be repeated.

The remedy of specific implement is rarely sought in delictual actions. This remedy is used to enforce positive obligations, that is it is a court order to make the respondent do something. Conclusions for specific implement arise occasionally in connection with nuisance.

APPENDIX

SAMPLE EXAMINATION QUESTIONS AND ANSWER PLANS

Question 1

Bill is the manager of a foundry. He hears cries and a commotion coming **A–01** from a part of the foundry 100m away. When he goes to investigate he discovers that there has been a spillage of molten metal and sees two men wrapping a third in a fire blanket. He can see that the victim's clothes are burning. He does not recognise the victim since his face is badly burnt and his hair has gone. He is screaming. At that point a crucible fractures and Bill and the two helpers spring away. The eruption of molten metal engulfs the original victim who burns to death. It dawns on Bill that the victim is his brother-in-law. As a result of the incident, Bill suffers clinical depression and insomnia. When he does sleep nightmares awaken him.

The foundry owners admit that the incident occurred as a result of their negligence, but they deny that they owed Bill a duty of care in respect of psychiatric harm. Can Bill recover damages?

Notes for answer

Clearly Bill has suffered loss in the form of a recognised psychiatric illness, **A–02** so the requirements of *Simpson v ICI* are satisfied. The real issue here is whether Bill should sue as a primary or a secondary victim. Since both appear possible from the text, you should consider both possibilities and evaluate Bill's chances of recovering damages in each.

Bill's best chances of recovering damages are if he can establish himself as a primary victim to whom a duty of care to guard against personal injury was owed. Applying *Page v Smith* he can do this if he can show that he was within the area of potential harm. The facts are very similar to *Campbell v North Lanarkshire County Council* so he should at least be allowed to lead evidence to show that he was in danger.

If Bill fails to have himself regarded as a primary victim then he must claim as a secondary victim. To recover damages he must satisfy the rules laid down in *Alcock v Chief Constable of South Yorkshire*. Clearly, Bill was present during the second incident and witnessed the immediate aftermath of the first with his own senses. Bill must prove close ties of love and affection with his brother-in-law and he will have to lead evidence to prove this. *Alcock* shows that such ties will not be presumed in this type of relationship. You might conclude that the requirement of a close tie of love and affection presents a barrier to recovery as a secondary victim that does not apply to Bill's case as a primary victim.

Question 2

A–03 Harry burns rubbish in his back garden every week at irregular times. The prevailing wind blows the smoke into Jessica's house whenever she opens her windows to air her rooms. Jessica claims that the washing hung out on her clothes line often smells of smoke and her white sheets are spoiled by sooty deposits. She has often complained to Harry.

Advise Jessica on any remedy she may seek. How would you advise her if a valuable damask table cloth has been ruined?

Notes for answer

A–04 Jessica may seek to interdict Harry from burning rubbish in his garden or, given that interdicts must be framed no more widely than necessary to obviate the harm complained of, she may seek to interdict him from burning rubbish in such a way as to cause nuisance. An interdict could be framed in terms that restricted Harry's burning to certain times or perhaps when the wind was not blowing towards Jessica's property. Jessica is more likely to succeed with this than an attempt to stop the burning outright.

To obtain any remedy Jessica must establish nuisance. She must establish that the harm or inconvenience complained of is *plus quam tolerabile* (more than reasonably tolerable) in the circumstances. *Watt v Jamieson*, 1954 S.C. 56 must be cited as laying down this requirement. The court has to balance Harry's right to do on his land anything that is lawful against Jessica's right to the comfortable enjoyment of her property. Disturbance must be serious, inconvenience substantial, in other words Jessica must show that the harm is material and given the facts this ought to be the likely outcome.

Jessica may be advised to seek damages in respect of the damask table cloth. It is important to note that, in addition to establishing nuisance, she requires to establish *culpa* where damages are sought on the authority of *RHM Bakeries Ltd v Strathclyde Regional Council*, 1985 S.L.T. 214. Fault in nuisance may be relevantly pled in terms of a deliberate act done in the knowledge that harm will be the likely result (*Kennedy v Glenbelle*, 1996 S.C. 95). Harry has been specifically informed of the damage his activities are causing so he has that knowledge and his persistence is culpable. Since *culpa* can be established Jessica should have her damages.

Question 3

A–05 Wullie steals a pig from Bob. Because Wullie does not secure his gate properly the pig escapes from his garden and runs across the road just as PC Murdoch is cycling past on his way to work. The pig knocks Murdoch off his bicycle. Murdoch is uninjured, but the bike is badly bent.

Murdoch gives chase to the pig to try and catch it before it reaches the street market and causes havoc. When the pig runs across the next road Murdoch is running so fast that he can't stop himself from running in front of an oncoming car. The driver, Daphne panics and steers her car into a lamp post.

Meanwhile the pig has entered Horace's garden and by the time PC

Murdoch arrives Horace has killed the pig with a live mains cable with which he is working. He tells Murdoch he did this to protect his cat which is curled up asleep in Horace's airing cupboard at the time of the incident. Viewing the death of the pig from over the hedge is Maggie, a vegan. Maggie suffers post- traumatic stress disorder from viewing the incident.

Consider the prospects for the parties involved of receiving compensation for their losses or injuries in damages.

Notes for answer

Damage to the bike: There is no liability under the Animals (Scotland) Act **A–06** 1997. There is no attack and, while pigs are foraging animals, the damage does not occur in the course of foraging. Moreover the damage is not to land or produce. Any liability will therefore depend on the common law. Wullie would be the person to sue, his status as keeper under the Act is irrelevant, but without his negligence in failing to shut the gate the incident would not have happened and clearly Bob is neither at fault nor involved in the chain of causation. The question of Wullie's liability to Murdoch turns on whether Wullie owed a duty of care to road users in the vicinity to secure the pig. Should an accident of this nature have been foreseeable to Wullie? Quite possibly.

Damage to the car: Murdoch in crossing the road owes a duty of care to Daphne. It is foreseeable that if you run out into traffic cars may have to swerve and damage may occur. Arguably, the standard of care on Murdoch may be lower than normal, though in the absence of an emergency this is not a very strong contention. *Gilfillan v Barbour* may be considered. It seems most likely that Murdoch will be liable to Daphne and if so his employers will be vicariously liable. The facts leave little scope for debate on this point. There is some suggestion in the text that damages may be reduced for contributory negligence. Any action brought by Daphne against Wullie should be ruled out on grounds of causation. If Wullie was negligent in failing to secure the pig this was not the direct or immediate cause of Murdoch running into the road having made his own decision to chase the pig so any causal chain starting with Wullie is broken. In any case, While Wullie may have owed a duty to road users and pedestrians in the vicinity of his house it must be doubtful whether this would extend to people using roads further away.

Death of the pig: Bob as owner has a prima facie case against Horace for the destruction of his property. Horace's potential defence under s.4(1)(iii) of the 1987 Act should be considered. This is the defence of acting to protect livestock and as it happens the cat does count as livestock for purposes of the defence (s.4(6)). Horace however fails to satisfy s.4(4) since he has no reasonable grounds for apprehending an attack on the cat. Bob therefore will get his damages.

Maggie's PTSD: Maggie is in no danger herself and so must be classed as a secondary victim. *Alcock* rules must be satisfied if she is to recover damages. She is present and the event and witnesses it directly, but unless she can establish close ties of love and affection with the pig she will get no damages if she sues Horace.

INDEX